TRUSTING GOD:

The Ultimate Peace

SEVEN SECRETS TO TRUSTING GOD

Trusting
GOD:

The Ultimate Peace

Seven Secrets to Trusting God

Raymond Ho

Destiny Image® Publishers, Inc.
P.O. Box 310
Shippensburg, PA 17257-0310

"Speaking to the Purposes of God for This Generation
and for the Generations to Come"

ISBN 0-7684-2169-1

For Worldwide Distribution
Printed in the U.S.A.

This book and all other Destiny Image, Revival Press, MercyPlace,
Fresh Bread, Destiny Image Fiction, and Treasure House books are
available at Christian bookstores and distributors worldwide.

For a U.S. bookstore nearest you, call **1-800-722-6774**.
For more information on foreign distributors, call **717-532-3040**.
Or reach us on the Internet:
www.destinyimage.com

DEDICATION

Over the years, I have been richly blessed to have served with so many wonderful people who have great faith in God. It is their absolute trust in God through a deep understanding of His Word that has inspired me to follow in their footsteps and devote my life to serving God.

I dedicate *Trusting God: The Ultimate Peace* to five great men of faith whom I have had the privilege to know and work for:

Pat Robertson, founder and chairman of the Christian Broadcasting Network.

Dr. Larry Ward, founder of Food for the Hungry.

Pastor Tommy Barnett and Pastor Matthew Barnett, cofounders of the Dream Center.

Robert W. Johnson, founder and chairman of Dominion Sky Angel.

These men are pioneers in their work who are having a profound influence on the lives of people across the nation and around the world. All have founded ministries that have had significant impact on the Kingdom of God. They have made this a better world!

CONTENTS

AN EXCERPT FROM
MY SPIRITUAL JOURNAL

Dear Child:

Do not doubt, do not question, do not be dismayed, for I AM FAITHFUL. That is why throughout the ages, men have turned to Me—because I AM TRUSTWORTHY.

In times of testing and trials, you will experience My faithfulness. You will find miracles at your lowest point, because that is where I show My power to those who trust Me.

Therefore, if you have arrived at your lowest point, you will find Me waiting for you. I have never left you or abandoned you.

When you can find Me and TRUST ME at your lowest point, then you have developed GREAT FAITH. That is when you KNOW GOD.

Therefore, do not curse the low points—they will mark the high points in your testimony. It is in the valleys that I forge your character.

Do not despair when you can't see how all My plans come together for good. I understand your feelings of helplessness.

TRUST ME and anticipate the GOOD I am about to release into your life, then you'll see how all the pieces fit together.

I promise you this: You will not be humiliated. I will move to raise your hope. I will see to it that LIGHT will shine through for you at the end of your dark tunnel. I will move mountains because I will not test you beyond your ability to bear.

TRUST in My goodness, TRUST in My sovereignty, TRUST in My power, TRUST in My mercy, TRUST in My deliverance, and TRUST in My love.

You will SEE all the attributes of God when you learn to TRUST ME while others give up.

Therefore, DO NOT GIVE UP YOUR TRUST IN ME. If you do, you will have nothing to trust and nothing to hold on to.

I alone am totally TRUSTWORTHY.

INTRODUCTION

AWAKENING THE DIVINITY WITHIN YOU

——• **The kingdom of God is within you.**
(Jesus Christ—Luke 21:17b) •———

*What do you do when the walls protecting you
begin to crack and crumble?
Where do you go when everything around you
turns to sinking sand?
Who do you turn to when the relationships you
depended on are severed?
Who do you trust in your darkest hour,
at your deepest depth, and in your most despairing moments?*

Trusting God: The Ultimate Peace offers provocative and perceptive solutions to these perplexing and painful questions. It presents seven secrets to trusting God and how to be trusted by God. They reveal timeless spiritual principles that can unlock the secret chambers of your heart, allowing you to take the journey within to approach God for divine guidance for your life.

It will help you tap into the cosmic wisdom of the ages and awaken the life of God within you. Then you will gain the enlightenment to cope, the knowledge to overcome, and the power to conquer the enemies of your soul that block the path to your sacred destiny.

Once you discover the "divinity" within you, there is no limit to your potential to be fully "human." There is no telling what you can accomplish when you know that the Creator of the universe is your partner. You are unique and distinct, a miracle that will never be repeated again. There is much more to you than you ever dare to think; it is waiting to be discovered inside and longing to be released.

This book is about trusting God: the one and only God. He is the Creator of the Jews, Christians, and Muslims. He is the Creator of all peoples and all nations. He alone can help you fulfill your true destiny. You will never know what heights you might soar until you learn to trust Him and spread your wings and fly like an eagle.

Today, seekers are full of religion but hungry for God; believers are constipated with man-made rituals but starving for spiritual reality. They long for truth that enlightens but resent religion that frightens. They are craving the healing hand of God but fleeing the pointing finger of pulpit masters.

People resist religion that is aloof, abstract, and lifeless, but long for genuine spiritual experiences that can satisfy the insatiable vacuum in their souls. They want relevant answers to their personal issues and practical solutions to the problems of daily living.

GOD-KEEPERS OR GATE-KEEPERS?

The true purpose of any religion is to point the way to God—the source of truth. Ideally, religion helps people learn the truth and live in love, peace, and harmony. At its worst, it separates, segregates, and serves its own selfish interests. Their leaders would rather see themselves as "God-keepers" than "gate-keepers," whose purpose is to point the way to God's presence.

This book is not about religion. It is about finding peace with God and in our relationships. It presents spiritual truths that help you blow away the mysterious fog surrounding spirituality and cut through the impenetrable veil of religiosity, tailored by a religious system that is often alienated from the ways of God.

It is written in simple language without being simplistic; short without being shortsighted. The purpose is to assist you in the discovery and application of these practical principles in everyday life.

Religion teaches people to seek God's approval through good deeds. In their desire to obey God, believers are taught to rely on self-determination, willpower, and discipline; to resist temptations and endeavor to perform diligent service.

Trusting God: The Ultimate Peace shows a different course—it leads you down the road where you can discover the God who can perfect you in obedience through His Holy Spirit. You become God's partner and collaborator, so He can perform good works through you and give you the strength to overcome temptations.

> *When you learn the secrets of trusting God, you will rely less on your own strength and depend more on His power. Through humble surrender and personal submission, you exchange the pride and guilt of religion for the love and grace of God.*

This results in the ultimate peace!

WE ARE TRUSTING EVERY MINUTE

Every minute of the day, we place our trust in someone or something, whether we are conscious of it or not. From the time we get up to the moment we fall asleep, we put our confidence in something outside of our control.

We trust our alarm clock to wake us in the morning. We trust the people at the electric plant to do their job while we are asleep, so the clock will go off as planned. We count on our car to start when we turn on the ignition, so we can get to work on time. We depend on our job to be there, so we can take home a paycheck to support our family. But when the system breaks down, our trust is shaken, our confidence shattered, and our faith strained by unexpected circumstances and unforeseen adversity.

Some time ago, I was the CEO of the Dream Center—a mega-church and humanitarian organization that was featured on the front page of the *New York Times* twice in a year during my time there. President George W. Bush visited us during his Presidential campaign and praised our programs at a press conference there.

I was recruited by the founder to strengthen its financial bottom-line and in less than six months, the $1.4 million debt was eliminated. But when the tide of recession swept across the global economy, it was time to "downsize." Several of the senior managers lost their jobs; but to my amazement, even my CEO job was eliminated!

The paychecks ceased and the severance package failed to materialize. Worse than that, my savings of a lifetime also vanished because of a sinking stock market. I went from being a millionaire to near bankruptcy in less than a year! I had no money to send my daughter to the prestigious university where she had been admitted to the honors program.

In hindsight, I made two serious errors—I trusted too much in the security of my job and the strength of the American economy. This led me to invest heavily in the technology sector of the ever-rising stock market of the late 90s. It was the height of the "dot com era" and investors were optimistic about the "new economy." When the market rose, my investments soared, but when the economy faltered, I lost almost everything.

The final kicker came when Bank of America and Macy's called to tell me I was months behind on my bills though I had no accounts with them. When I checked with the credit bureaus, I discovered the shocking news that a perpetrator had stolen my identity. He was approved for a mortgage loan in my name and was having quite a shopping spree…for several years!

Sometimes in life, when it rains, it really pours!

LIFE IS FULL OF SURPRISES

When you live long enough, you'll know that life is full of surprises. It's a long and winding road, and you never know exactly what is around the bend. There are times when the journey feels like being strapped in a roller coaster with blindfolds on.

Just when we thought the world had entered into a new era of peace and prosperity after the collapse of communism, another war had only just begun—the war on Terrorism. Now we face invisible enemies spreading the threat of hijacking, suicide bombings, bioterrorism, nuclear terrorism, and terror of all kinds.

One thing is for sure: the cycle of war and peace, boom and bust, prosperity and recession, is the only certainty we can count on in an uncertain world. Consider the corporate scandals and bankruptcies of such giants companies like Enron and their impact on employees, suppliers, and stockholders. Then there are the unpredictable natural disasters—earthquakes, hurricanes, tornadoes, floods, and landslides, ravaging entire communities and cities throughout the world.

Every day, terminal illness, cruel crimes, and senseless violence claim the lives of innocent victims. Every hour, thousands of faultless drivers meet their tragic death on the road because of drunken drivers. Every minute, reckless acts of infidelity, thoughtless deeds of ambition, and indiscreet words of anger separate close friends, destroy intimate relationships, and split up families.

According to a recent Gallup Poll, six out of every ten marriages will break up in this country; four out of ten kids will go to bed tonight deprived of saying good night to their biological fathers, spreading consequences throughout society.

A Cruel, Chaotic and Confusing World

Global threats, natural disasters, and personal tragedies like these make this a cruel, chaotic, and confusing world: a fearful place to live, a risky time to make lasting commitments, a dangerous environment to start a family.

With so many impending threats and invisible enemies lurking in our imagination, no wonder people have a hard time trusting anyone. They feel stressed and strained. Many get their release from alcohol and drugs; others find comfort in pills and visits to their therapist; some turn to religion for answers.

It is easy to give in to anger, sorrow, and despair when we face threats, hurt, pain, and loss. Engulfed by grief and sorrow, embittered by betrayal and humiliation, afflicted by trials and tribulations, it is natural to wonder: *Is there anything I can believe in? Is there someone I can depend on? Is there anyone I can trust?*

Trusting God: The Ultimate Peace guides you through the maze created by these perplexing questions of life. It shows you that in the final analysis, God is the only one you can trust.

True peace doesn't come from "positive thinking"; it is not based on a "good feeling"; it does not come from the absence of conflicts. The ultimate peace comes when we know God and His sovereignty. When we believe and trust God, we tap into the power of the divine life that grows within us.

When we know the strength and dependability of God's power,
it enables us to trust Him in spite of our trying circumstances.
This gives us an infinite source of hope and confidence,
a boundless feeling of comfort, security, and rest
that leads to the ultimate peace.
Trusting God gives us the ultimate peace

because of God's infinite power, unlimited strength,
and unshakable faithfulness.
He is never too busy to listen, too tired to pay attention,
or too weak to help in our time of need.
Even though the strongest and most loving people
in our lives fail at times, God never fails!

This revelation of God's dependability revives, restores, and renews our faith in God, in ourselves, and in humanity. It leads to peace with God vertically and peace in our relationships horizontally, resulting in the ultimate peace.

THE PURPOSE OF THIS BOOK

If you are seeking meaning, purpose, and direction for your life, *Trusting God: The Ultimate Peace* will help you find the narrow path to your destiny. If you are weighed down by worries, paralyzed by fear and given in to despair, it inspires you to pick up the pieces of your broken dreams, dust yourself off, and face life's challenges with hope again.

When you learn to trust God, He will show you the truth that sets you free; you will reject self-pity and refuse to see yourself as a victim of circumstances. When you tap into the hidden spirituality within, it will break through your defenses and denials, illusions and delusions...like dandelions through concrete.

Trusting God: The Ultimate Peace is about letting go of fears: fear of approaching God and what he might require of you; fear of who you are and who he is; fear of love and change; fear of failure and death.

When you learn to trust in God's perfect,
steadfast, and eternal love,
you develop a consistent faith
and persistent hope that conquers your fears.
Love is the antidote to fear
and perfect love is the panacea for all fears.

Trusting God opens the eyes of your spirit and the ears of your heart, so you can acquire the spiritual vision to see, the sensitivity to hear, and the passion to follow God's plan for your life. Then you will attain the insight and foresight to see beyond your present circumstances, and go around whatever mountains that block the realization of your divine destiny.

WHAT ARE YOU FACING?

Are you facing a difficult trial? Are you up against an impenetrable wall? Have you given up on your dreams? Have you hit rock bottom? Are you at the point of no return?

Then know this: *If you think you are seeking God, the good news is God is seeking you!* He has been drawing you to Him all along, waiting for you patiently with His arms stretched out, if you would only trust Him and reach out your hands. *You can cast your cares on Him because He cares for you.*

I am speaking from personal experience, having been lost for 40 years without a personal relationship with God. During all that time, I struggled on my own, climbed up to the top of some of the highest mountains, and camped down in some of the lowest valleys in my life. I did everything on my own strength, trying my best to control my own destiny through determination, perseverance, and hard work.

For thirteen years, I was the CEO of two public television networks and served three governors, including Bill Clinton. We won dozens of prestigious awards along the way, including many Emmys, and I was featured in numerous papers, magazines, radio and television networks. I appeared on the cover of *The Washington Post* and was honored by *Esquire* as "one of the men and women under forty who are changing the nation."

But without God, I was lost and miserable inside!

While I was considered "successful" in the eyes of the world, I never experienced peace in my life. I suffered loss, survived pain, and endured humiliation. I persevered through the trauma of divorce and the breakup of my family. I walked through the pain of separation from my daughter and the death of my father. I persisted through months of sleeplessness because of a constant back pain from a traumatic car accident.

After my spiritual awakening, I faced religious persecution, false accusations, and betrayal by ambitious associates that ended my public television career. For the first time in my life, I had to contend with the humiliation of unemployment.

But through trusting God, I always bounced back stronger, wiser, and without bitterness in my heart.

I started a new career in ministry serving God by helping people in need. I became a vice president at CBN—the Christian Broadcasting Network; I served the poorest of the poor around the world at Food for the Hungry; I became the CEO of the Dream Center and City Help Inc. in Los Angeles.

Then God miraculously opened a door to the world of television again. I became the Vice President of Marketing at Sky Angel—the only Christian organization in the world that is licensed by any government to own and operate a multi-channel, direct broadcasting system that is capable of reaching the whole world with the Gospel!

Through it all, I learned a priceless lesson—God understands our suffering and He is always there beside us. We are not alone! We can always trust Him as He gives us inner strength even in the eye of the storm. God never promises that the journey will be easy, but He assures us that He will be there with us throughout the journey to help, teach, and perfect us.

Remember, *a diamond was once a chunk of coal that was perfected under pressure.*

LIFE IS A JOURNEY

Life is a journey and God is always there with us: in good times and bad, in prosperity and times of need, in victory and defeat. I discovered that *God delivers us in the furnace, but not from the furnace of life's afflictions.*

It was during these intensely trying times that God taught me the "secrets" of trusting Him and the ultimate peace that comes with it—a peace that is beyond understanding, more precious than money, power, position, fame, security…or anything in this world!

I faithfully kept track of God's communications in 13 spiritual journals during a ten-year period and received priceless spiritual revelations along the way. It is the contrast between God's wisdom and my foolishness, His faithfulness and my fickleness, His strength and my weakness, that inspires me to share what I have learned through this book.

Therefore, I dedicate this work to God and to all of you who want to learn how to trust Him, with all my love.

In my last book *Hearing God: The Ultimate Blessing*, I shared the secrets of how to "hear" God—how to plug in, turn on, tune in, listen, hear, and obey Him. The purpose was to inspire readers to seek an omnipotent, omnipresent, and omniscient God to receive divine guidance for their lives.

In Trusting God: The Ultimate Peace, the goal is to encourage and empower you to trust an all-loving God. The objective is to assist you in discovering the divinity within, as you exercise your faith to take the journey into the secret chambers of your own soul.

No matter what circumstances you are in, whatever mistakes you have made, there is no way you can ever stray too far from the reach of God's tender love and mercy. You can always turn to God because He is all around you, He is in you, and He is waiting patiently for you.

That is why trusting God is the path to your ultimate peace!

CHAPTER 1

IN GOD WE TRUST

> The significant problems we face cannot be solved at the same level of thinking we were at when we created them.
>
> (Albert Einstein)

If you want to trust God…

Secret # 1:   Seek to know God first. You can't trust someone you don't know. Knowing about God is not the same as knowing God.

> *When you seek Me, you will find Me.*
> *When you find Me, you will know Me.*
> *When you know Me, you will love Me.*
> *When you love Me, you will trust Me.*
> *When you trust Me, you will discover*
> *My divine presence within you.*
> *Then you will experience God*
> *and find the ultimate peace.*

There are no secrets to trusting God,
trusting God is the secret.

(An excerpt from my spiritual journal)

NOWHERE TO TURN, NOWHERE TO HIDE

Where do you turn when you are surrounded by evil? What do you do when your back is up against the wall? Where can you go when there is no way out? Who can you trust when death is staring you in the face?

On the morning of September 11, 2001, the Twin Towers stood tall, rising majestically over the skyline of New York City. It was the beginning of a new day, a morning like any other. The alarm clocks went off and New Yorkers got out of bed, had breakfast, and saw their children off to school. Thousands strolled into the lobbies of the North and South Towers after getting off the subway, lined up at the elevators, and packed the offices of the 110-floor buildings at the World Trade Center.

Suddenly, an incredible explosion shook the walls of the building as if a giant bomb had gone off. When people realized a jet plane had crashed into the side of the North Tower, total panic set in as thousands ran for their lives in all four directions, screaming as they ran for cover. People fought their way down elevators and stairways while some escaped out the lobby, looking up in dismay, only to see a scene from hell!

Minutes later, a second hijacked plane slammed into the side of the South Tower, exploding into a mighty fireball! Glass, burning debris, and pieces of flying metal from the plane rained down like gigantic hailstones in a bad nightmare. Desperate victims hung out the windows of the burning buildings with hands reached out, grasping for a miracle; some finally gave up after their bodies caught fire and dived to the concrete pavement below. Moments later, the buildings collapsed one after another, exploding into a gigantic black mushroom of dirt, dust, and darkness!

As Americans watched this horrific live coverage on television, another evil plot was brewing on a third hijacked plane headed for Washington, D.C. Within minutes, American Airline Flight 77 smashed into the massive Pentagon, crumbling its impenetrable walls, scorching everything in sight, turning the complex into a virtue war zone!

While carnage spread in New York City and Washington, United Airlines Flight 93 was 35,000 feet in the air over Pennsylvania. At 9:15 a.m., according to the transcript of the cockpit radio transmissions, a voice screamed, "Get out of here! Get out of here!" A fourth group of terrorists hijacked the plane and cold-bloodedly stabbed some of the passengers with knives.

This four-man suicide squad was headed for another strategic target, perhaps the White House, the Capitol Building, or Air Force One. But some brave Americans stood in their way and resisted their captors. As a result, Flight 93 dived into a field, gouging a huge hole in the ground near Shanksville, Pennsylvania, killing all the terrorists, crew, and passengers.

THE POWER OF A PRAYER

While others were seized with fear and paralyzed by panic, what gave these men the courage, boldness, and audacity to perform such a heroic act? The clues to the answer may be found in a phone call.

Todd Beamer, 32, an executive with Oracle, Inc., tried to call his wife, Lisa, on the airphone. His credit card was rejected so he got a GTE operator instead. As the passengers screamed in the background while one of them was being stabbed to death, Beamer made a moving request to the operator to pray the Lord's prayer with him.

Together, they reached out to God: "*Our Father who art in heaven, hallowed be Thy name. Thy kingdom come, Thy will be done in earth, as it is in heaven...and deliver us from evil: for Thine is the kingdom, the power and the glory, for ever. Amen.*"

When they were finished, Beamer asked the operator to call his wife and two young sons to tell them he loved them. As the phone dangled from the seat, the operator heard his parting words, "Are you ready guys? Let's roll!"

For evil to triumph, all it takes is good men standing by and doing nothing. The valiant decision and selfless acts of these courageous Americans saved the lives of many, and may have altered the future course of American history. We will never know what might have happened if evil had had its way that fateful day.   •

In his most desperate moment, Beamer made another call through prayer: *As a child of God, he called 911 on 9/11 and asked for his Father in Heaven*. He trusted God to hear him, just as God had heard Jesus at the Garden of Gethsemane before He faced execution on a cross. In the face of death, Beamer tapped into an inner strength that comes only from trusting God. He drew from it the moral strength, courage, and fortitude to fight back and overcome evil with good.

Like Jesus, Beamer knew he was not going to get out of this situation alive, but God gave him the extended spiritual vision to see beyond his present circumstances so he could say, "Thy will be done on earth as it is in Heaven." He had a glimpse from the eyes of eternity and was no longer afraid of his destiny—he saw where he was headed so he knew what he had to do.

Beamer was comforted after his prayer and was reminded that in the final analysis: *God is the only one he can **trust** because His word is his bond and His promises are true*.

And God promised in His Word:

> *The Lord is near. Do not be anxious about anything, but in everything, by prayer and petition, with thanksgiving, present your requests to God. And the **peace** of God, which transcends all understanding, will guard your hearts and your minds in Christ Jesus* (Philippians 4:5b-7).

Beamer trusted in God's Word and His sovereignty—He is in control even in the midst of chaos and crisis, distress and destruction. He was assured that God's purpose will prevail and good will ultimately triumph over evil.

That's why he had the audacity to say, "Let's roll!"

You too can access this invisible spiritual world—you can learn to approach God to receive guidance, peace, and comfort, for the cares and crisis in your life. But you don't have to wait till the day of your disaster.

THE AMERICAN SPIRIT

These four men did not die in vain; instead they became an inspiration for other Americans at one of the darkest hours in our nation's history. All the world's darkness cannot snuff out the light of a single candle—in the heart of tragedy, love shone through and hope prevailed.

Among the smoldering ashes of disaster, hundreds of fire-fighters, police, paramedics, and volunteer rescue workers unselfishly gave their own lives to save the lives of others. They went into hell and back at Ground Zero, searching through the fiery wreckage and smoldering rubbles day after day, hoping to find just one more survivor beneath the carnage.

Their unwavering courage and steadfast dedication symbol-ized the indomitable spirit of America—the land of the free and home of the brave. In the midst of grief and anger, Americans turned to God and rediscovered their spiritual roots and heritage. In the face of evil, they rose to their finest hour with their spirit of caring and giving.

A new spirit of patriotism and unity emerged across the land. Stars and stripes appeared everywhere—from the mountains to the prairie, from the White House to the crack houses. "God Bless America" and "United We Stand" became the rallying cry of the American people.

What gives Americans this invincible spirit in the midst of death, destruction, and disaster? Is it our freedom? Is it democracy? Is it our history? Is it our values? Is it our faith?

It is all of these and more. It is a spirit of hope that comes from a deep and abiding *trust* in God as a people and a nation. That is why the United States of America is the only country in the world that clearly acknowledges God on its currency since 1864. America is proud and bold in declaring who we trust. Imprinted on American currency is the statement: *In God We Trust*.

Next time you take out a quarter or a dollar bill, take a look to see for yourself, then stop and ask, "Why does it say, *In God We Trust?*"

EVERYBODY NEEDS SOMEBODY

Everyone wants to have someone in their life whom they can trust. We all desperately need a person we can turn to when faced with difficult decisions we have to make, or when we are overwhelmed with the struggles of life.

Trust is a tricky thing though; finding someone who will listen and support us is not easy. Allowing someone to enter into the secret chambers of our heart is a very scary thing, especially when we have been betrayed in the past. But everybody needs somebody in their lives. Everyone needs to trust someone sometime. Finding that "somebody" is the real challenge.

God is that "somebody" for your life. He cares deeply for you and is interested in the most detailed aspects of your life. He stands at the threshold of your soul, hoping for an invitation to enter in to be with you. He wants to listen to the sorrows of your heart and hear the dreams of your life. He is not mute. He is patiently waiting there to communicate with you.

You can learn to connect with this invisible spiritual world, the parallel "secret Kingdom" where God lives; it is here that you can discover solace for your sorrow and solutions for your suffering.

I have a question for you: Do you know this God? Do you want to know this God we trust?

YOU CAN'T TRUST SOMEONE YOU DON'T KNOW

If you want to *trust* God, you have to *know* Him first. Knowing about God is not the same as knowing God. The difference between knowing about God and knowing God is like the difference between an astronomer and an astronaut; astronomers study the stars while astronauts go there and visit them.

> *Knowing about God comes from*
> *secondhand knowledge from others;*
> *knowing God comes from receiving wisdom,*
> *knowledge, and understanding directly from Him.*
> *Knowing about God is an intellectual exercise of the head;*
> *knowing God is a spiritual experience of the heart.*

Too many seekers are more concerned with explanations of "what God is" rather than experiences with "who God is." It is not "what" you know that will help get you through the toughest trials in life; it's "who" you know.

You cannot *know* God until you have *experienced* the truth of God in the *reality* of everyday life. This only happens when you make a commitment of the heart and the head, exercising both faith and reason to open your life to the possibility of discovering Him as He draws you near.

During a prayer and meditation session, God explained it to me this way:

> *When you seek Me, you will find Me.*
> *When you find Me, you will know Me.*
> *When you know Me, you will love Me.*
> *When you love Me, you will trust Me.*
> *When you trust Me, you will discover*
> *My divine presence within you.*

> *Then you will experience God*
> *and find the ultimate peace.*
> *There are no secrets to trusting God,*
> *trusting God is the secret."*

THE KINGDOM OF GOD IS WITHIN YOU

God is omnipresent. His spirit is everywhere so He is also deep within you. If you want to find God, don't look for Him around you, look for Him within you! As Jesus said, "The kingdom of God is within you" (Lk. 17:21b).

Begin the journey inward and move deep into the recesses of your own heart; through prayer, fasting, and meditation, you will find the path that leads to His presence. It will lead you to the place where you will find answers to your most perplexing questions. Living in the presence of God changes you and the focus of your life. You will experience a metamorphosis of your heart so you will want to love, care, and help others in need.

When we receive revelation knowledge from God, it enlightens our thinking. It is as if a light is turned on in the darkness of our inner life. It opens the eyes of our soul to see and understand the truth of God. The brilliance of this blinding Light reveals truth and convicts us of error, but it also blinds us to our senses, self-centeredness, and selfishness.

In that moment, our spiritual blinder is removed. Suddenly we know that we *know* the truth! We have awoken to the realization that our perceptions are tainted with the restrictions of our transient mortality. They are only perceptions of the truth, based on our imperfect knowledge and inadequate experiences, which are filtered through our prejudices and desires.

Only the whole truth, and nothing but the truth, can set us free from our flawed feelings, erroneous perceptions, and infected images of reality. It is this truth that sets us free from the prison of our own erroneous thinking and leads us down the path to find our ultimate peace.

A seeker who wrote this old hymn said it best "Once I was lost and now I am found! Once I was blind, but now I see! Once I was bound, now I am free!"

MY FIRST ENCOUNTER WITH GOD

For my first 40 years, I knew *about* God but I never knew Him. I grew up in a Catholic family in Hong Kong. And then, during my first marriage, I converted to Judaism for 16 years to become a part of a Jewish family in America. It wasn't until April 17, 1992 at 3:00 a.m. during my second marriage that I truly "experienced" God for the first time. That night I had a spiritual encounter like Saul had on his journey to Damascus—I heard the audible voice of God for the first time.

This brief encounter with the "living" God was my "born-again" experience. It was the awakening of my "higher" self, my "real" self, the Spirit of God within me. It saved my marriage and changed the course of my life forever! After that night, I knew the difference between knowing about God and knowing God.

This experience propelled me into an inspired devotion for the next ten years to try to understand the secrets of this invisible world. I gave up a successful career in television and began my spiritual journey in search of the treasures of the Kingdom.

I began to pursue God with the passion of a lover, the discipline of an athlete, and the intensity of an explorer. Every day, my soul sought after Him like the deer longs for water on a hot summer's day. I desperately wanted to experience God's presence again because I so relished the peace I had tasted that night. It was a peace that was beyond description, the kind of peace that had eluded me all those years.

When God communicated with me during my prayer time, I consistently captured everything down in a spiritual journal. I faithfully meditated on the meaning of what I heard, and willingly attempted to obey the instructions I was given. On many occasions, because of my stubbornness, I had to learn the same lessons over and over again, until at last, the truth was internalized and integrated into my life.

Knowing God is a journey of a lifetime; it takes faith, time, and commitment—faith to learn and trust His Word, time to develop and grow the relationship, and a commitment to love and obey Him.

HOW DO YOU KNOW GOD?

How do you know a God you can't see?

Fortunately, God has revealed Himself to us throughout the ages. He communicated through the prophets in visions, dreams, miracles, and the spoken word. Their stories and experiences help us to understand who God is and how He works.

While every religion teaches believers about the truth of God, He is not real until they have personally experienced the reality of God. Religion is man's best attempt to explain the nature of God; but because God is divine, transcendent, and supreme, it is impossible for any man-made religious system to define and confine God.

Explanations about God must be empowered by experiences with God. It is not enough to fill our minds with knowledge concerning God. The intellectual knowledge must be transcended by personal experiences with God. The Scriptures can give you direction *and* lead you to an intimate encounter with God.

There are many ways to know God. Reading about other peoples' spiritual experiences can provide clues for your own spiritual search. Their discoveries will create greater spiritual hunger in your own life.

God reveals Himself to us in many ways. Too often our focus is placed on seeking external evidence for God, when we should be turning inward. Knowing God in the inward way will demand that you learn to quiet yourself and open your heart to Him. You must learn to shut down the internal noise on the surface of your consciousness and tune in to your heart. God is there and He will reveal Himself to you. God is a loving God and He loves to reveal

Himself. The challenge is to rise above all the distractions keeping us from hearing and seeing Him.

The spiritual pioneers who have gone before us believed that God communicated His will and nature through the prophets and then in the sacred Scriptures. They all believed that God's Word is truthful and infallible. That is why we can trust God's Word.

I believe that God's Word is trustworthy because it has been tried, tested, and proven true through time and history. The words are our Creator's standard operating manual for mankind, capturing what the Spirit of God communicated to man and equipping us for godly living.

The Bible is a collection of books reflecting God's revelations to man through 40 authors, in three different languages, over 1500 years. It is not just a collection of stories, fables, and myths, but a historical document and a masterpiece of inspirational and prophetic literature.

Scriptures are accurate, authoritative, and time-tested throughout the ages. That is why these sacred books are the most read and revered text in history of civilization. They provide inspiration and guidance to men in leadership positions for all generations.

The Founding Fathers of America Knew God

The founding fathers of the United States of America knew God and drew inspiration from the Bible. On the Fourth of July, 1776, Congress issued the Declaration of Independence. It stated:

> We hold these truths to be self-evident, that all men are created equal. That they are endowed by their Creator with certain inalienable rights, that among these are life, liberty, and the pursuit of happiness.

James Madison, the chief architect of the American Constitution wrote:

> We have staked the whole future of American civilization, not upon the power of government, far from it. We have staked the future of all of our political institutions upon the capacity of each of us to govern ourselves according to The Ten Commandments of God.[1]

Benjamin Franklin spoke these immortal words:

> *I have lived long Sir, and the longer I live, the more convincing proofs I see of this truth—that God governs in the affairs of Man. And if a sparrow cannot fall to the ground without His notice, is it probable an empire can rise without His aid?*[2]

Then, he moved that prayers be said at the Convention, asking for the divine help of God.

George Washington, the first President of the United States of America wrote this in his prayer book:

> *Direct my thoughts, words and work. Wash away my sins by the immaculate Blood of the Lamb, and purge my heart by Thy Holy Spirit. Daily frame me more and more into the likeness of thy Son Jesus Christ.*[3]

Since then, every U.S. President begins their presidency by swearing an oath of office with their hand over the Holy Bible. Later, during their term of office, they each had the opportunity to place their trust in God during the most crucial times of their presidency.

Abraham Lincoln faced a Civil War and a nation coming apart at the seams. Franklin D. Roosevelt fought a World War with Nazi Germany and the Japanese. John F. Kennedy confronted the threat of communism. Jimmy Carter faced an Arab oil crisis. George Bush fought the Gulf War, and his son George W. Bush leads a war on terrorism.

Every new American citizen is required to "pledge allegiance to the flag of the United States of America, and to the Republic for which it stands—one nation under God, indivisible, with liberty and justice for all."

And every witness testifying in our American court system must first confess, "I promise to tell the truth, the whole truth, and nothing but the truth, so help me God."

THE AMERICAN DREAM

Much has changed since the days of the founding fathers, and some lament that Americans have drifted far away from their roots. But the United States of America remains a godly nation because a silent core is still committed to obeying God and living out the ideals that made this nation great.

Americans are a people tied together by the power of ideas. We believe in the dignity of the human being; we believe in political, economic, and religious freedom. These ideas have power because they are founded on fundamental truths based on the Word of God.

America is great because it attempts to do what is right by the Word of God, and God has "blessed" America! It is the strongest and most prosperous nation in the world today and it is seen as the "land of opportunity" by peoples all over the world.

That is why every year, over half of a million people immigrate to America. It is the last place of refuge for the tired and weary—people fleeing political persecution and tyranny from their own country and hoping for a better life and a brighter future.

America still opens its arms to welcome everyone, regardless of their race, color, or creed. Almost anyone who aspires to live the "American dream" can be an American. One basic requirement is that they be "of good moral character."

At the heart of the American dream is our hope in God, at the core of our American strength is our reliance on God, and at the source of our American confidence is our trust in God. That is why the American dollar—the most *trusted* currency in our world today—proudly pronounces, *"In God We Trust."*

But we cannot *trust* what we do not *know*. We cannot simply rely on our statements of truth. We must *experience* the *reality* of the words we declare.

Endnotes:

1. James Madison as cited by Gary DeMar, *God and Government: A Biblical and Historical Study,* (Atlanta, GA: American Vision Press, 1982), pp. 137,138.

2. Benjamin Franklin as cited by James Madison, *Notes of Debates in the Federal Convention of 1787*, (New York: W.W. Norton and Co., 1987), pp. 209,210.

3. George Washington as cited by W. Herbert Burk, B.D., *Washington's Papers*, (Norristown, PA: published for the benefit of the Washington Memorial Chapel, 1907), pp. 87-95. Quoted in LaHaye, *Faith*, pp. 111-113.

CHAPTER 2

GETTING TO KNOW YOU

> ———• Our seeking of God is not all a matter of
> our finding him…
> It is rather a quieting and ordering of our whole
> life by self-denial, prayer, and good works so that
> God himself, who seeks us more than we seek him,
> can "find us" and "take possession of us."
>
> (Thomas Merton) •———

If you want to trust God…

SECRET #2:   Get to know God through His Word, then
experience Him through His Spirit.

WHOM CAN YOU TRUST?

If we could choose just one person to trust, wouldn't it make
sense to pick someone who has the desire and power to help us?
One who accepts us for who we are, and recognizes the deepest
desires of our hearts? A friend whom we are certain will always

be there whenever we need comfort? One who will never abandon us in our time of need?

There is only one who can meet all these conditions:

He is God!
He is our loving Father watching over us in Heaven.
He is our best friend walking with us on earth.
He is all-knowing and understands
the deepest thoughts and desires of our heart.
He is all-powerful and can protect
and care for us in times of need.
He is always present and is available to us
wherever we are, and whenever we call on Him.
He is almighty and supreme so He can never fail.
That's why we can trust God!

WHY IT IS TOO HARD TO TRUST

As children, we are perfectly trusting in the beginning. We
trust our mother and father and believe that they will always be
there for us. Unfortunately, parents get divorced and eventually
they grow old and die. The pain of losing parents through divorce
or death strikes a severe blow at our ability to trust.

As teenagers, we "fall in love" for the first time and trust our
lover. Disappointingly, when the infatuation passes and the relationship ends, our hearts are broken again. Eventually, most of us
find the "right" person to marry. Although we start out with
mutual trust, regrettably, too many marriages end in divorce,
leaving partners abandoned, depressed, and all alone. Our ability
to trust is diminished once again, making us more cynical and
skeptical about trusting anyone.

We trust our employer to provide security for our family and
the government to give benefits for our retirement. But in times
of economic instability, we are either laid off or our benefits and
salaries are slashed. And when we thought we could trust in our
friends and relatives to lend a helping hand in our time of need,

we discover how many real "friends" and "relatives" we really have.

Finally, we are certain we can at least trust our own children when we grow old. But sooner or later, they leave home to pursue their own life and careers. They start their own families and we are left all alone, isolated, and disillusioned again.

So whom can we trust? Is there anyone who won't abandon us? Is there someone who will not consider us a burden or an imposition? Is there someone who will always be there for us, when everyone and everything else has disappeared?

In the final analysis, you will discover that God is the only one who is totally trustworthy. He will not disappoint you because He never fails. He is the only one who will be there when everything else has dribbled out of your hands. He will be there always, even as you face the darkness of death because He is God!

When the trials of life shake your belief system to the core, and the shock of unfortunate circumstances crushes your spirit until you've run out of strength and hope, remember you can dial 911 for help. As a child of God, you can always turn to your Father in Heaven because:

> *The Lord is the everlasting God,*
> *The Creator of the ends of the earth.*
> *He will not grow tired or weary,*
> *And His understanding no one can fathom,*
> *He gives strength to the weary*
> *And increases the power of the weak.*
> *Even youths grow tired and weary,*
> *and young men stumble and fall;*
> *But those who hope in the Lord*
> *Will renew their strength.*
> *They will soar on wings like eagles;*
> *They will run and not grow weary,*
> *They will walk and not be faint.*
> (Isaiah 40:28b-31)

If we want to approach God for help, we must learn to trust Him and surrender our adult cynicism and skepticism. We must restore our childhood innocence and capacity to trust and believe. Jesus said, *"Unless you change and become like little children, you will never enter the kingdom of heaven"* (Mt. 18:3b). He was teaching His disciples to approach God with a humble and teachable spirit—like a needy and trusting child.

FACING THE STORMS OF LIFE

When the storms of life rob us of our peace, and the hour of calamity, catastrophe, and chaos saps us of all strength, remember God is waiting for us to call. He wants to help renew our strength and restore our peace. We are not an imposition on God. He encourages us to approach Him, *"Come to Me, all you who are weary and burdened, and I will give you rest"* (Mt. 11:28). And He promised, *"Ask and it will be given to you; seek and you will find; knock and the door will be opened to you"* (Mt. 7:7).

But first we must learn to TRUST God, then we must demonstrate FAITH and ASK for His help. If we want God to help us, we must first BELIEVE and acknowledge that HE IS GOD, and He is willing, able, and ready to help us.

God doesn't want to make us feel any worse than we already feel about our desperate situation before Him. He promises to bless us in spite of our predicament:

Blessed are the poor in spirit, for theirs is the kingdom of heaven. Blessed are those who mourn, for they will be comforted (Matthew 5:3-4).

God alone can provide the constancy we need in our vacillating and precarious world. He is the only one who is permanent in a shifting society. He never changes. He is the same yesterday, today, and forever!

That is why throughout history—in every culture and civilization, no matter how primitive or sophisticated—man has always reached out to God to find his source of strength and tower of trust.

Reaching Out to God

Ancient civilizations reached out to the invisible world of the gods searching for security, stability, and the meaning of the human condition. The Egyptians, Greeks, and Romans invented numerous gods to fill those needs, and many elaborate myths emerged to help people relate to these gods.

For example, the Greeks worshipped Zeus, and believed that he was the king of all their gods who lived on the sacred mountain of Olympus. The Olympic Games today come from the ceremonies that were held in his honor. Athena was his daughter—the goddess of wisdom, courage, and victory. Apollo was his son and the god of light; Aphrodite was the goddess for love and beauty; Ares was the god of war. The Romans had similar gods with different names: Jupiter was the king of gods; Mars was the god of war; Venus was the goddess of love…and the list goes on.

Man has always felt a need for an external spiritual aid to direct his hollow world. To fill that need he has turned to the imaginations of his mind, creating images that would give significance and support to his feeble existence.

Then God revealed to the Hebrews that there was only ONE God and He is the God of everything! He made Himself known by speaking through His prophets and revealing Himself through human events, so man might *know* and *experience* Him. Through Moses and the prophets, God gave the Ten Commandments and the law; through Jesus, He showed us how to relate to God and man.

How Do You Trust an Invisible God?

To trust, you must first get to know the object of your trust. Trust is based on a firm belief and confidence in the substantive nature, integrity, and reliability of the person or thing we trust.

Trust requires faith, and faith needs a foundation to stand on. Our intimate knowledge and understanding of the person is the foundation for this faith, and it only comes through time. It is not enough to have *explanations* of God, we need personal *experiences* with God; it is only through those divine encounters that we develop a strong basis for trust in Him.

Trust in a relationship grows only when that bond between two parties is tested through time. With the passing of time, trials will test and strengthen that relationship. Then a proven loyalty develops into an "intimacy" that gradually matures into this special state called "trust." To develop trust, we must first reach out and fully commit ourselves to "knowing" the person we seek to trust.

Getting to Know You

In the classic 1956 Rodgers and Hammerstein's musical *The King and I*, the king of Siam and the British teacher Anna got off to a shaky start. Even though he hired her as the teacher of his children, he couldn't trust her because he didn't know her. He had only heard about her qualifications through others.

As an Asian, I must explain that the East is different from the West and the cultures are dissimilar. In the same way, God is distinct from man, even though man was created in His image. His thought processes are different than ours and His ways of doing things are often opposite to what we expect.

Anna and the King were separated by a gulf of varying cultures and customs, and because of these differences, they encountered misunderstandings that undermined their ability to trust—the basis for intimacy in any relationship.

Everything changed with time, when they got to know one another through *experiences*. It is the same with God. If we want to know Him, we must come into His presence and experience Him. We can only trust something we know and we can only know what we have experienced.

Getting to know God is the first step towards trusting Him. It is a step-by-step, day-by-day process. The more time you spend with God, the more intimately you will come to know Him. Then you will feel a sense of inner peace and personal freedom in His presence.

Unfortunately, there is a lot of misinformation out there about the character of God. Some portray Him as a powerful judge; others display Him as a callous legalist. It is only as you have your own experiences with God that you discover the warmth of His love and the sweetness of His presence.

You will experience a free and easy feeling in His presence because of His unconditional acceptance and affirmation of you just as you are—a child of God who is perfect in His sight. The warmth of His love helps you draw near to Him and feel an unexplainable pleasure in His presence—a new sense of well-being that is beyond any joy you have ever known. You will feel connected and confirmed by the wealth of the beautiful and new things you are learning about Him day by day.

When you get to know God, you will love and trust Him. You'll discover that He is the one you've been looking for all your life!

CAN MAN REALLY *KNOW* GOD?

God is divine and infinite; man is mortal and finite. God is spirit and man is flesh. Can man really know God? Fortunately, God has always reached out to man in a committed effort to communicate with us so we can fellowship with Him. He reveals Himself in five different ways so that He can be *sure* that we can *know* Him.

1) He breathed into each of us a *spirit*, a portion of the essence of His nature that enables us to communicate with Him spirit to spirit. We all have the same spiritual equipment and capacity to hear and experience God.

2) He placed a *conscience* in each of us, a moral compass that knows innately the difference between good and evil. No matter what nation, tribe, or tongue we come from, we share an innate sense of morality of what is right and wrong. It is built into the human being at birth. For example, we know that lying is wrong, stealing is bad, and murder is evil, no matter how primitive or sophisticated a society we come from.

3) He revealed His will and nature through His *Word*. He gave the Ten Commandments in writing as a moral code to guide our conduct and provided Scriptures through the prophets with illustrated examples of what to do and what not to do, in every situation we might face in life. He laid out the consequences of each action so there would be no confusion or ambiguity about His will.

4) He appeared in the form of humanity through His Son Jesus Christ to show "the way the truth and the life" (see Jn. 14:6). Through the sinless life of Jesus Christ, He gave us a *perfect role model*.

5) He sent His "Holy Spirit" after Jesus returned to Him so we can each have our own private *counselor*, *teacher*, *and guide* for continuous support from Him. This enables His Word and direction to be always fresh, timely, and relevant to our daily lives.

GOD'S WORD IS TRUTH

God is trustworthy because His Word is truthful. He is trustworthy because He is faithful to His promises, like a good friend or a loving spouse. But the difference is this: God's faithfulness is so perfect, His Word is so absolutely dependable, and His promises are so irrevocable, that even when we break our promises to

Him, he does not break His promises to us. His Word is eternal and unchangeable.

> *God's Word is true and truth is eternal,*
> *immutable, forever, and transcendent.*
> *It is independent of what we think.*
> *Truth is true even if no one believes in it;*
> *a lie is false even if everyone swears by it.*

If the written Word of God is the complete operator's manual for life, then the spoken word of His Spirit is the personal help we can receive from God directly through His customer service hotline. Consider if your computer is frozen and you face an urgent deadline: Would you comb through the thick manual or call the customer hotline?

While we can overcome many of life's challenges if we conduct ourselves according to God's written instructions, He also knows we have constant need and dependence on Him for personal direction and in times of trouble. That is why He sent His Holy Spirit to be our counselor and companion throughout our journey.

MAN TRUSTED SATAN'S LIE

Scriptures explain how the crafty serpent deceived Adam and Eve into disobeying God in the Garden of Eden. They trusted satan's lie and ate the forbidden fruit from the tree of the knowledge of good and evil. This original sin caused the fall of man and so he was banished from the presence of God.

Since that day, man has bought into satan's lies as truth. Once people are deceived into thinking that his lies are the truth, they will do everything in their power to defend what they think is "truth."

The best lies are usually based on distorted truths; they are counterfeit truths. But a half-truth is not truth, and two half-truths do not add up to a whole truth; they still equal a lie!

Truth is light that exposes darkness and reveals sin; it convicts the sinner and condemns the sin. The sinner defends himself by turning everything around and accusing the one who is telling the truth as the liar, traitor, and sinner. Therefore, the truly honest person must be stopped, and if he does not cease telling the truth, he must be destroyed. He must be cast out of sight, so the sinner can continue to live comfortably with his sin, which is based on a lie. This is how satan's deceptions work.

Like a stubborn teenager, man has refused to listen and obey God's truth, except during periods of great hardship and suffering. He has insisted on going his own way, worshipping idols—the gods he creates to serve his own desires so he can enjoy his "freedom" from God. He has continually persecuted, tortured, jailed, and executed God's prophets.

Originally created in the image of God and given dominion to rule over all of God's creation, man has never lost his desire to regain his "paradise lost." Man still wants to be God—to rule over his own life and to accumulate the wealth and power to dominate others.

But after the fall and the resulting separation from God, man has been subject to errors, illusions, and delusions. This makes him increasingly vulnerable to satan's lies, which deceive him into hearing what he wants to hear and seeing what he wants to see, when it suits his selfish pride.

WHY GOD CAME INCOGNITO

After the death of the prophet Malachi around 430 BC, God was so angry with the rebelliousness of man that he stopped speaking through prophets. He was so distressed by man's stubbornness and refusal to listen that he kept silent for the next four hundred years!

But it was always the purpose of a loving God to bridge the gap between God and man, so He sent His Son Jesus to be the "bridge over troubled waters." He left the glory of Heaven and descended into the depths of man's despair. He stepped out of the spirit world and entered into the physical world, taking on a fleshly form.

God came incognito, hidden as a common carpenter named Jesus. He didn't come as a king, as many had hoped, because He wanted the average man to identify with Him.

He fulfilled his age-old promise to the Jews to send a "Messiah" or Savior to set them free from the errors of their ways and to deliver them from the penalty of sin. Through Jesus, God provided the anecdote for sin and its consequences—a divine prescription that would heal the incurable state of pride and rebellion that separated us from a holy God.

God expressed His love in a way that even the simplest of man can understand throughout the world and through all time. In every culture and every race, people understand the love of a father for his son, especially if it is his *one and only* son. So God chose to express His perfect love by coming in the form of Jesus—His only Son, His own flesh and blood, and the most precious part of God Himself. He sacrificed Him to pay the penalty for our sins, so we can appreciate the immeasurable depth of His love and be reconciled to Him.

God is as loving as He is just. His perfect love is giving and forgiving, but His absolute justice requires complete fairness and impartial judgment. Otherwise, there would be no standards for good or evil, right or wrong, and no accountability.

God's Word Is His Bond

All Scripture is "God-breathed and is useful for teaching, rebuking, correcting and training in righteousness" (2 Tim. 3:16). God made it clear in His Word: The result of obedience is life and blessings. His great desire is that we come into union with Him where our wills are one with His will. He wants us to have an abundant life and a prosperous journey on earth and an eternal home in a state called Heaven.

The consequence of disobedience is curses and death—a state of separation from Him called hell. The condition of "sin" is when we miss the mark, wander off the path, or go over the edge of God's will. Sin is choosing something other than His perfect will for our lives and thus creating a conflicting condition that separates us from God. Sin is rebellion; it is obedience gone bad because of erroneous thinking, and it causes pain and suffering.

God instituted judgment not because He wanted to harm us. Suffering serves as a mirror so we can see the consequences of our own actions; it is a tool for our own learning and correction. Without justice, there are no consequences for our actions, good or evil. Justice says, "You will reap what you sow"; God judges us by what we have done and repays us according to our deeds.

God's Word is His bond; it is consistent, reliable, permanent, immutable. It is truth that never changes regardless of our fluctuating perceptions; God never goes back on His Word. That is why God's Word is totally reliable and trustworthy. That is why we can always trust God!

Even if He wanted to forgive us for our disobedience, He would not cancel the penalty of sin because it would violate His own word. It would be totally inconsistent with His nature—His holiness, righteousness, justice, and absolute perfection.

Now the real dilemma emerges. He knows we can't change ourselves—we do not have the power to make the changes. An error is incapable of correcting itself.

That is why God came up with the ingenious plan to "save" us by paying the penalty for our sins Himself through Jesus. His sacrifice of His holy body and the shedding of His sinless blood served as the cover for our sins. Then God could remain consistent to His word, stay true to His nature, and still redeem us to Him.

It is when we receive God's precious gift of Jesus that we are saved and reconciled to our Father in Heaven. Then we can *experience* God through our "awakened spirit"—the life God begins to grow within us. There is nothing we can do to deserve this because He has already paid the price. We simply accept this priceless gift of grace and mercy through faith.

THERE IS A CATCH

There is a catch to all this. God gave us free will to choose as His highest expression of love and trust in us, but that is a double-edged sword because it gives us the freedom to make our own decisions and be held accountable for them, for good or evil.

Therefore, even this free gift of salvation is only going to those who trust God enough to receive it on faith. God is not a benevolent dictator; He won't force it on us against our free will, for that would violate His loving nature.

God's Word is truthful because it is tested, tried, and true throughout the ages by man's experiences. It can be temporarily hidden as the clouds of circumstances pass through our lives; it can be twisted and distorted by satanic deceptions and misguided men; but it never changes and it can never be destroyed because truth is eternal!

If God's Word is true and truth is eternal, then time will always defend and testify to the faithfulness of His Word.

For example, the Roman authorities and Jewish religious leaders at the time were threatened by the "truth" as proclaimed by Jesus. They humiliated, persecuted, tortured, and executed Him and His followers, in an attempt to kill the "truth."

But time demonstrated the truth of God's Word because Jesus was resurrected from the dead, just as He said He would be. He was sent by God and He is the Son of God. He came to reconcile us to our Father in Heaven and awaken us to the truth that we are all children of God.

Eventually, even the Roman Emperor Constantine, the most powerful human being of his time, knelt before the cross of Jesus Christ and acknowledged God's truth. He became a Christian and the truth spread throughout the Roman Empire and the whole world.

That truth remains true two thousand years later. Every president of the United States—the most powerful leader of the most powerful nation in the world today—is sworn into office with his hand over the Word of God—the Holy Bible.

Even our definition of time in the entire world today—no matter what country you are in, what language you speak, what religion you believe in—is tied to what Jesus did on the cross. This is the year 2003 A.D. because it is two thousand three years after His death.

This does not prove the validity of God's Word; it merely confirms the truth.

If you haven't read and explored the truth of God's Word, start today. Get to know Him by reading the sacred Scriptures then open your life to Him and be prepared to experience God in very personal and unique ways. It will set you free and change your life forever!

IS FAITH BLIND?

When you read Scriptures, you'll discover that God performed many miracles that validated that Jesus was not only the messenger of God who came to teach us, but also the Son of God who came to save us. He performed many miracles because God always accompanies His message with power; there are signs and wonders that validate their messengers.

God did not ask man to cast all reasoning aside and blindly believe Him. He demonstrated the true identity and divinity of Jesus through these miracles. He turned water into wine, multiplied loaves of bread and fishes, walked on water, healed the sick, opened the eyes of the blind, made the lame walk, gave hearing to the deaf, and raised the dead.

Even after witnessing firsthand such amazing miracles, Jesus' apostles failed to fully recognize the true reality of Jesus. The glory was concealed in the cloak of His flesh and they were unable to perceive the "treasure hidden" in the vessel.

But God understands the weakness of our faith. Jesus was not only resurrected from the tomb, but He returned to appear to His disciples for 40 days to prove, beyond the shadow of a doubt, that He was, and is, God!

When Jesus ascended to Heaven, He sent His Holy Spirit to come upon His followers at Pentecost to give them power and the courage to testify to the truth. Once truth was revealed, nothing could stop these men—not beatings, imprisonment, hunger, torture, lions, fire, or execution. After they knew that Christ was always going to be with them, and that they had eternal life, even death could no longer frighten them.

Because He lives, He is here for you. He is one of us. He knows the pressures of living in the flesh and the stresses of living in the world. In fact, He suffered more than anyone on earth for our sins, so He understands our pain and suffering. That's why we *can* trust Him!

How Can a Man Be God?

Like the Jewish religious leaders of Jesus' time, you might ask, "How can a man be God? It is totally incomprehensible, incredible, and unbelievable!"

You are right, it's all of these things. But if you ask the wrong question, you will never find the right answer.

The question isn't, "How can a man be God?" but "Can God come in the form of a man?"

The truth is—God can do *anything* He chooses! He has always worked through people.

God is Spirit and man is flesh. If God never spoke to man through His prophets to reveal who He is, we would never be able to comprehend Him. If God never came in the form of humanity, we would never be able to understand and identify with Him. He spoke His word through the prophets but demonstrated truth and grace through Jesus; He gave the law through Moses, but He fulfilled His Word through the life of Jesus.

Seek the Truth Yourself

If you want to know God, seek the truth yourself. Don't be content to simply read the spiritual experiences of others; become a pursuer of God. Start by reading the Scriptures and set aside time to communicate with Him. But first, shut down the clatter of the internal noise in your soul, open your heart, and listen for the still small voice of God and He comes to talk with you.

He will reveal the truth to you. He will show you the awesome plans He has for your destiny.

God alone can draw you to Himself and reveal His unfailing love: Jesus is the greatest testimony of God's love for you and His greatest gift to you. When you willingly accept His precious gift, sincerely acknowledge the truth of Jesus, turn from your sins, and invite Him into your heart, you will instantly be reconciled with God. It's that simple!

Then His Holy Spirit will reveal to you great and unsearchable things about Himself. He desires to hear the whisperings of your heart. He will give you the capacity to know Him and the faith to trust Him. He will awaken the divinity within you and help you live the abundant life that He has planned for you.

I am speaking from firsthand experience. He did that for me and he will do the same for you because He loves you. He is love. That is His nature and He cannot respond to you in any other way.

I have been in the television industry for 25 years; I trust God like I trust my television: Not only because it is always there, but because of what I can see through it. I trust God, not because of what He did in the past, but because of what He is doing in the present. I trust Jesus, not because of the miracles He performed during His lifetime, but because of the miracles He is accomplishing in my life right now!

Napoleon said it best when he described Christ: "I know men, and I tell you, Christ was not a man. Everything about Christ astonishes me. His spirit overwhelms and confounds me. There is no comparison between him and any other being. He stands single and alone."

CHAPTER 3

CAN'T BUY ME LOVE

⟶ **A man is a slave to whatever has mastered him.**

(Apostle Peter—2 Peter 2:19) ⟶

If you want to trust God...

SECRET #3: Put God first and give up the idols in your life. Then He will give you the desires of your heart.

MONEY, MONEY, MONEY!
You can never be too rich, you can never be too thin, you can never have too much power...so goes an E-trade commercial on television.

The Beatles' song, "Money," describes the prevailing life philosophy of many people today when they said repeatedly,

"Just give me the money, that's what I want!"

The lyrics in this song and the lines in the commercial tell us a lot about our popular culture today. They are a reflection of the idols of our time—the false gods we have come to love and worship in a materialistic and hedonistic society.

We worship at the feet of these idols because they promise to give us what we want, but they are not gods and they have no power to help us. They are counterfeit gods we've created in our imagination; they are extensions of our selfish nature that seeks its own way and desires to fill its life with "things."

So what's wrong with desiring "things"? What's the harm in having a few idols to entertain us?

The problem is this: *Though we create idols to serve us, we instead become slaves to the idols we created. Idols are addictive; whatever we "must have" ends up having us.* We become subservient to these false gods and they pull us further and further away from the *real* God.

An Unholy Altar of Seduction

Every day we are flooded with an endless torrent of slick TV commercials, radio spots, billboard signs, magazine copies, and advertising slogans. They appeal to our pride of life and feed the lust of our eyes. They promote messages like, "You're somebody who has arrived. You need this product to prove it and you deserve it today!"

This stream of memorable slogans penetrates our consciousness and seeps into our soul as it magnifies its power over us. We sit passively under its reeducation as we are taught what to value, what to desire, and what to trust.

The television is the master teacher of our civilization today. It is on seven hours and twenty minutes a day in the average American home. People worship daily at the foot of this unholy altar of seduction while they find it hard to find an hour to worship God at church on Sunday.

Advertising-supported mass media relentlessly peddles products and services that magnify the idols of our time—money, power, beauty, fame, and "success." They promise instant answers to all our deepest desires, miracle cures, and wonder drugs that overcome every problem in our lives. All this time, the messages pound their subtle doctrines into our collective sub-consciousness, teaching us what we should covet in life, what we should set as goals, and what directions to pursue in our dreams.

As a result, people in our consumer society today spend an exorbitant amount of time and energy pursuing money and buying things that promise to satisfy them. They relentlessly pursue power hoping it will make them feel important, secure, and in control of their destiny. In the end, they are deceived and enslaved by these transient idols they worship.

It is ironic that many spend their entire lives acquiring, accumulating, investing, and multiplying the idols of money, power, and fame, only to face the reality of having to leave everything behind to someone else eventually. And everything they accumulate passes to people who never had to work for it.

Naked we came from our mother's womb and naked we depart—we can't take anything with us!

You Can't Take It With You

I can tell you a few stories about how the treacherous idol of money ruined the lives of people on both sides of my family. I have two grandfathers and four grandmothers—my two Chinese grandfathers each had two wives simultaneously, not to mention the concubines. This was both culturally acceptable and perfectly legal back in the early 1900s.

In fact, the wealthy Chinese gentlemen were only taking their cues from the emperor himself. He had thousands of wives and concubines tucked away in The Forbidden City. Their highest hope was to be chosen to sleep with the emperor, and their greatest dream in life was to bear him a son. With such tough competition, sleeping with the emperor was like winning in roulette, and bearing his son was equivalent to hitting the jackpot in Las Vegas!

At one time, my grandfathers were both very wealthy—one inherited his money and the other made it; one had old money, the other had new money; one blew it all, and the other hoarded it all.

As the old saying goes, "If you make money your god, it will plague you like the devil." In the end, both were deceived by the seductive and addictive power of money.

Ho Chak Lam was my dad's father; he never worked a day in his life. He never had to because his family owned more land than the eyes can see. He was known as "the rice king" in a southern province of China in the early 1900s. Rice was the "white gold" of its day, creating a pathway to power and prominence.

Sadly, money ruined my grandfather. He was a handsome-looking man, an eastern Clark Gable who grew up to be the notorious playboy of his time. He was educated and intelligent, raised by private tutors. But the seductive power of money allowed him to indulge in just about every vice that is known to Man—drinking, gambling, opium, womanizing…you name it, he did it!

When I was growing up, I noticed he was missing a part of his little finger. During an infamous gambling incident while my grandfather was under the influence of alcohol, he gambled away much of the family fortune over a cricket fight.

After he sobered up, he was terrified that his father might cut off his inheritance. He cleverly staged a dramatic scene before the whole family and shockingly chopped off part of his little finger to pledge that he would never gamble again. And he kept his oath! But regrettably, the enticing idol of money just led him on to the next vice—opium, the drug of the rich!

Grandfather was always extravagant. He would send one of their three ships to the closest city to pick up the latest western invention known as "ice cream" for my dad. Without refrigeration, it became soggy by the time it arrived; but dad didn't know better—it was his first experience and he licked it to the last drop. Every time the merchants heard the horns of my grandfather's ships blowing while pulling into the harbor, they would automatically raise their prices.

When the communists swept over China, my grandfather's family narrowly escaped to Hong Kong in the middle of the night. A former servant tipped them off the night before the army came to ravage the compound. They confiscated everything and tortured those who were left behind; rich landowners were forced to kneel on pieces of broken glass. Some chose to jump into a well to avoid the agony.

Family members grabbed what they could and ran for their lives. There was no way to take much of anything with them so most everything was left behind. All the land that the eye could see and generations of family inheritance vanished from my family in one night!

Life is truly unpredictable. There are times when you can't take anything with you, not even during this life!

Money Can Give You Grief

Wong Yui Nam was my mom's father. He was a very successful self-made man. He cofounded the China Motor Bus Company in Hong Kong—the mass transportation of that bustling city for almost a century. His public corporation was the equivalent of a top Fortune 500 company in the U.S. He made a fortune in his lifetime, but money didn't bring him everything he had hoped for. In fact, the idol of money led to much grief in his family.

Grandmother was a Catholic whose mortal sin was her inability to bear a son for my grandfather. She did her best and became pregnant six times, but gave birth to all girls! So Grandpa took on wife number two and she hit the jackpot with three sons...and three girls!

Maybe that explains why poor Grandma became a devout Catholic who took communion almost every day for the rest of her life until she died at a hundred. She was seeking for something, or should I say "someone," to ease the pain of rejection in her own life.

Chinese fathers rejoice when they have a son to pass on their family name, but even sons can become a curse instead of a blessing if they are corrupted by the idol of money.

My grandfather's youngest son was kidnapped by abductors. They cut off one of his ears and sent it with a ransom note to my grandfather to get his attention. But Grandpa loved his hard-earned money more than anything in this world; instead of paying the ransom, he reported the incident to the police and never saw his son again.

Another son grew up to be a playboy and alcoholic because money gave him the freedom to do so. At an early age, he was addicted to women and alcohol and walked around with a hard liquor bottle in his hand all day long. The alcohol eventually ate away at his kidneys, and one fateful day the pain became so unbearable that he jumped off a skyscraper and ended his life.

Money is a seductive idol but it is also a ruthless master. In the end, it plunges man into ruins and destruction!

WHO IS YOUR MASTER?

Jesus said, "No one can serve two masters. Either he will hate the one and love the other, or he will be devoted to one and despise the other. You cannot serve both God and Money" (Mt. 6:24).

The apostle Paul said, "The love of money a the root of all kinds of evil" (1 Tim. 6:10a).

Money itself is not evil; it is neutral in its value. It can be used for good or evil, depending on who controls it and for what purpose it is used. But when the love of money becomes the magnificent obsession in our lives, it becomes an idol—a false god that will eventually lead us down the path of death and destruction.

When we position *anything* above our love for God—money, power, position, fame, pleasure, security, nature, freedom, self, and even our work for God—it eventually becomes another idol.

In the first commandment, God clearly states, *"I am the Lord your God...You shall have no other gods before me."* (Ex. 20:2-3),

In the second commandment He says, *"You shall not make for yourself an idol in the form of anything... (Ex. 20:4)."* For our own good, God strictly forbids the worship of idols.

Why did God forbid the worship of idols? Because they are not gods; they have no power; they are not sovereign over the affairs of man; they can neither save nor deliver. They are false gods—futile creations of a selfish, materialistic imagination. Those who worship idols forfeit the grace of God.

Throughout the history of civilization, man created all kinds of idols in the form of gods and goddesses to suit his own needs and desires. There were the gods of the sun and the moon, goddesses of the earth and fertility, gods of fire and war, goddesses of love and beauty, gods of the sea, trade, travel...covering every aspect of life.

Why Does Man Desire Idols?

Why does man have a desire to create idols? Why do people need a focus for their attention and worship?

First, man has an inner need to master his environment. His relentless pursuit of knowledge, science, and technology is an attempt to explain and control the physical world around him; this gives him a certain measure of security and peace. But man is also a spiritual being and has a deep desire to interpret the human condition and the nature of who he is.

How did we get here? Who created us? Why are we so different from all the other animal species? What is the meaning of life? Where do we go when we die? Is there a life after death? Why are things the way they are in nature? Who created the galaxies and the universe?

The answers to these perplexing and self-penetrating questions can only come from the Creator of the universe. God reveals the answers through His Word in Scriptures so man can understand.

God is spirit and because we are created in His image, we too are spirits. He created man with a body for him to live in during his journey on earth and breathed into man His essence—His spirit. As the spirit entered the body, man became a living soul with a mind, a will, and emotions.

Our spirit is the eternal part of us that cannot die because it is not physical, but metaphysical. We have part of God's spirit within us creating a connection with God, enabling us to hear and communicate with Him.

We are eternal spirits traveling in our bodies during our brief time on earth called life. From the perspective of eternity, our brief experience on earth is very short—like flowers that fade and grass that withers; a mist that lingers for a moment and disappears.

Man is God's highest creation; we are children of God with His spiritual DNA. Made in His image, we have divinity within us and were given the authority to "have dominion" over all His creation (see Gen. 1:28 KJV). We were created to be God's representatives, to rule over His kingdom.

WHY DID SATAN DECEIVE MAN?

Imagine this scene: Day after day, the Morning Star, the Chief of Angels leads multitudes of angels to sing and worship God in the perfection of His holy presence in the heavens. Pride ultimately drives him to mobilize a third of the angels to mount a rebellion against God. He wants to be like God and be worshipped. He wants to BE GOD!

God casts him and the rebellious angels out of Heaven; he becomes satan the devil. He becomes the archenemy of God; his anger, jealousy, and bitterness have been brewing ever since.

So when God created man to worship and fellowship with Him and gave him dominion over everything on earth, you can imagine how satan felt. He saw man as the usurper of his heavenly position. His ultimate revenge against God was to take man down with him to hell, where he reigns.

If man won't worship him voluntarily because he is evil, then satan will devise a plan where he will be worshipped one way or another, even if it means enslaving man through deception.

Satan's plan was, is, and always will be, to appeal to man's pride. His scheme is to deceive man into doubting God's Word and His goodness. Then he promises him seductive idols that can help him "be like God." He deceived Adam and Eve and tempted them with the fruit—the first idol. It promised "the knowledge of good and evil" so they could "be like God" (see Gen. 3:5).

Satan used the powerful lure of pride to deceive them into thinking they could do without God once they ate the forbidden fruit and gained the "knowledge of good and evil." He promised them that once they were equal to God, they could be "free" from God's control.

This caused the original fall of Man, but satan is still succeeding today with the same time-tested plan. He promises man everything he wants in the form of idols, enticing him to be "free" from God.

MAN'S GREATEST DILEMMA

Ever since the fall, man has been trying to regain his original "divine" status, just as the fallen Morning Star never really gave up his desire to "be God" and be worshipped. Man has a need to worship idols because they present to him the false promise to return to his "paradise lost."

One of the biggest lies that the devil propagates is, "When I get everything I want, then I'll be happy." This is another way of saying, "When I am God, I will be satisfied."

My wife and I know a Beverly Hills couple who own one of the most fabulous collections of rare Ferraris in the world. They live in a magnificent mansion with a palatial garage that can accommodate a small fleet. But their six-car garage is still not enough to store all 25 of their Ferraris! They rent space at the airport so they can easily ship their toys to the countries where they can exhibit their world-class collection.

We attended one of the competitions in Beverly Hills and were not surprised that their vintage 1950s Ferrari took the first prize. Then it occurred to me, the other 24 Ferraris and a house full of trophies must not have been "enough" to satisfy this couple; something kept driving them to strive for more.

One characteristic of idols is their addictive nature. When the Israelites came out of Egypt, it wasn't long before they returned to worshiping idols. After Moses had gone up the mountain for a period of time, they pressured Aaron to create for them an idol in gold, and they proceeded to worship this golden calf.

The Egyptians and Canaanites worshipped gods in the forms of a bull and a heifer because they were symbols of power, fertility, and prosperity. The idols held out the promise of distributing to them everything they wanted, which would enable them to "be like God" and be "free" from God.

In contrast, God's Ten Commandments seemed like a list of "thou shall nots" restricting their personal freedom. In reality God gave these moral laws as a fence to protect them from their fallen nature. The purpose was to make man less vulnerable to deception, sin, and rebellion—the lures of idols that would lead them away from God.

Worshipping idols is spiritual adultery
and those who cling to idols
detach themselves from the love and grace of God.

THE GOLDEN CALVES OF OUR TIME

Today, we have many idols in our modern civilization. Money is the most seductive; power is the most addictive; and "selfism" is the most popular.

Money is the golden calf of our time and the mother of all idols. It seductively promises the power and fertility to give birth to *all* the other gods we crave: power, position, pleasure, popularity, prestige, and possessions. Money is the most seductive idol because it appears as the elixir for all our desires and the panacea for all our problems. The obsessive pursuit of money eventually plummets man into destruction, for it leads to a litany of other sins: greed, jealousy, envy, covetousness, and betrayal.

Power is the most addictive idol; power corrupts and absolute power corrupts absolutely. When man thinks he can "be God," he is very dangerous. Fallen man is not capable of exercising such absolute authority without the guiding hand of God. Those who lust after power without God will eventually be powerfully destroyed. Just take a look in history at the ash-heap of dictators like Hitler.

The "Self-centered" Society

Today, the most popular idol is "selfism" because all the idols like money, power, pleasure, popularity, prestige, and possessions…all feed the ego and venerate the self. Our society is becoming more and more self-centered.

We revere personal freedom and choice, but reject personal responsibility and morality. We have bigger cars but smaller hearts, larger homes and a weaker conscience. We have discovered the marvel of splitting the human gene, but rejected the wisdom of the Ten Commandments. We remember lines from Hollywood movies but cannot quote verses from the Bible.

In the end, the Beatles discovered some truth as they concluded in their hit song, "Can't Buy Me Love" that "money can't buy me love."

The truth is: Money can't buy us love or any of the most precious things in life—like friendship, contentment, peace, integrity, character, or a good reputation. In the end, the measure of our life is not what we took but what we gave. You can't take anything with you!

Idols are seductive, addictive, and deceptive. In reality they are not gods—they are simply false gods! They are pathetic substitutes for the true joy, personal freedom, and ultimate peace that come from trusting the *real* God.

If you want the real God who has the power to help you, then put Him first and abandon the idols in your life.

One day, God explained it to me this way:

If you give Me your heart,
I will give you the desires
of your heart.
If you give Me your best,
you can expect My best.
If you put Me first,
I will answer you first."

CHAPTER 4

HOW BIG IS YOUR GOD?

> **Man's mind stretched to a new idea never goes back to its original dimension.**
>
> (Oliver Wendell Holmes)

If you want to trust God...

SECRET #4: Communicate with God; the more you know Him, the bigger He gets. The magnitude of your problems diminishes in comparison to the size of your God.

EVERYBODY HAS PROBLEMS!

Let's face it, everybody has problems! The longer you live, the more problems you'll encounter and the more complex your life will become. Life is full of surprises. It twists and turns like a river; and if you live long enough, you'll know that life has more twists and turns than a bag of pretzels!

People have all kinds of problems. Some face financial problems because of unemployment, bad investments, or their inability to control their spending. Others face relational struggles created by conflicts with their spouse, family, or coworkers. Some endure psychological problems because of severed relationships, divorce, or the resulting stress that comes from the breakup of a family. Still others are overwhelmed with feelings of guilt, shame, and loneliness.

These personal struggles are manifested with worry, anxiety, and sleeplessness as people strain to figure out the source of their dilemmas. Many face the internal agony of anger, jealousy, and bitterness thinking that life has somehow been "unfair" to them. Then there are those who don't know what their problems are, but live in a troubled world of discontent, emptiness, and purposelessness, never being able to track the cause of their pain.

Our world is not perfect and people are not always honest. Innocent people often get caught in evil circumstances that are not their fault. Good is not always rewarded and evil is not always punished, at least not in the timetable we expect.

So what is your response when you confront the tyranny of life's problems and crises? Who do you turn to when confronted with unsettling setbacks, disappointments, rejection, betrayal, or loss? Where do you go for a little tender loving care, personal support, affirmation, healing, and restoration that you so desperately need?

TO CHANGE YOUR FUTURE, CHANGE YOUR THINKING

The Chinese word for "crisis" is a combination of two characters that mean danger and opportunity. Is a crisis a danger or an opportunity? Whether it is a stumbling block or a stepping-stone depends on your perspective. Life is what we choose to make of it. It is a reflection of our thinking and the sum total of all the choices we've made up to this present moment.

If we want to improve our life, we have to refine the content and pattern of our thoughts; if we want to change our future, we have to alter the source and direction of our thinking. When we turn to God to enlighten our thinking, we tap into a fresh oasis of truth that gives us the necessary wisdom, knowledge, and understanding to do what is *right*. When we align our will to God's will and do what is right, we are *righteous*.

Trusting God is not surrendering the steering wheel of life over to God so that we do nothing but pray in the passenger seat. Faith without deed is dead; so even if you pray till the cows come home or fast till you look like a corpse, unless you accompany your thoughts with action, nothing happens. God gave us *free will* and appointed us to be the captain of our ship and the pilot of our life.

No one can change us except ourselves, and nothing can change us without our cooperation, not even God. To accomplish God's divine destiny for our life, we must seek direction from our Creator and become His true partner and collaborator, which requires humble submission, faithful obedience, patient cooperation, and an unwavering trust in God.

God loves and trusts us so much that He gave us free will to exercise this responsibility, but we are held accountable for the decisions we make and reap their consequences, for good or evil. Trusting God requires that we follow the details of the flight plan God has charted for each of us for our journey of life. If we run into turbulence, He promises we can always call for help and His Spirit will be available as our copilot with instructions to help us.

We can't choose our parents or the personality of our children; we can't do anything about the weather. There's not much we can do about the cards we are dealt in life, but we can choose how we play them. We can't always prevent the problems that come our way in life, but we can control our responses to them. We can't change our past but we can alter our future.

The God who created our mind, will, and emotions has the power to renew our thinking and change the course of its negative flow. As we submit to His awesome power, He can help us alter our internal view of ourselves and external view of the people around us. When confronted with life's situations, whether we see danger or opportunity, a stumbling block or a stepping-stone, depends on our thinking. The only thing that differentiates a problem from an opportunity is a judgment.

WHO CONTROLS YOUR SELF-IMAGE?

We alone control our self-image and determine our self-esteem. Otherwise it wouldn't be called *self*-image and *self*-esteem. Too often, we allow others to define who we are and thereby turn over the control of our lives to them. This is the result of flawed thinking that originates from erroneous precepts.

Scriptures say, "My people are destroyed from lack of knowl-edge" (Hos. 4:6a). Just as we can't fly a plane without a flight plan, we can't live a successful life without direction and instruc-tion from our Creator. Yet every day, we insist on doing it on our own, apart from God.

Let me illustrate this with an incident in my life.

My daughter Leslie was born prematurely, arriving a month early. When she came out, I thought my wife had given birth to a monster—she had no hair, no eyes, no nose, no face—just two giant cheeks! The doctor had earlier whispered the word, "breached," but I had no idea what it meant. Then when I saw those monstrous needles and giant scissors…I almost passed out.

After a traumatic night at the hospital, I came home exhaust-ed and drained, but I knew my wife would be extremely disap-pointed if the baby room wasn't ready when she came home. A man must do what he must do—so I faced my challenge of assembling the crib in a state of sleep deprivation. There was an instruction booklet that came with the giant box, but do you think I took the time to look at it?

I confess I am not the mechanical type, but it seemed simple enough. Don't tell me you need a college degree to put a simple crib together…besides I have two degrees! But I struggled for the next two hours, till the wee hours in the morning, and still couldn't get it together somehow. I cursed that crib like it was the devil, "This cheap piece of ——and ——, it must be defective! It's probably made in Taiwan, otherwise it's got to fit!"

Finally, after several rounds of man-against-crib, I gave up my pride. (You know that strange need that we men have to prove ourselves right, even if it makes us totally miserable.) I gave in and looked at the instruction booklet. It turned out I had the nuts and bolts reversed; it was a simple mistake that was easily corrected. My nightmare was finally over!

Don't Fall in Love With Your Blind Spots

All of us have moments like these when we allow our blind spots to block our ability to see the simple solutions to our problems. When we trust God, we trust our Creator to give us the proper direction and instruction for life. What better person to trust for explaining how to assemble that crib than its inventor? Similarly, who else can give us the answers to life's problems better than God—our Creator?

But to do that, we have to first dispose of our pride and turn humbly to God for help. The Bible is God's operating manual for man. It contains the solutions for life's perplexing problems, but God also gave us direct access to Him through His Spirit like a customer service hotline.

Prayer is our communication to God; meditation is our listening to God; and revelation is God's communication to us. It is His invitation to change and it requires a response from us.

God Talks to People!

I have news for you—you can talk to God and you can hear from Him. God *still* talks to people!

It's not news at all because God has *always* talked with people; this is how the prophets of old received their revelations throughout the ages. Because God is alive and not dead, He is still talking today. He has never stopped talking and He wants to talk *to* you and *with* you.

Some theologians try to convince us that God stopped talking after the Bible was completed, but we know differently. He continues to speak today, if only His children would listen. He will talk with you right now, if you learn how to plug in, turn on, tune in, and start listening and hearing Him.

God can communicate anywhere, anytime, and in any way He chooses. He wants to talk with His children so much that He will use whatever means possible to reach them; He will speak through ways that are most comfortable to them. He communicates through His written Word—the Scripture—or He can reach us directly with His spoken word through His Holy Spirit. He can speak to us through another person in our lives or through a line in a book, a movie, or a song. He can speak through His creation and reach us through nature with the delicate song of a tiny sparrow, a mysterious mist at dawn, or the spectacular colors of a rainbow.

In *Hearing God: The Ultimate Blessing*, I wrote about communicating with God and why it is so important that we learn to listen and discern the voice of God. When we hear God, we are blessed because He gives us the right perspective to see the truth and reality of our situation. Most of life's problems are caused by our failure to understand our predicament, so we end up in a dilemma not knowing what to do.

For example, God spoke to me when I was facing what I thought was an impossible situation. I had no idea what to do so I asked Him for help. Then He answered,

> *"When you face a mountain before you, look not at the mountain, but look up to God who created the mountain. If you meditate on the mountain, it will grow in size and appear overwhelming. But if you focus on God and understand why I have placed the mountain before you, it will strengthen your faith, and the magnitude of your problem will diminish next to the size of your God."*

WHY HEARING GOD IS THE ULTIMATE BLESSING

Let me share a personal experience to illustrate why and how *hearing God* is the ultimate blessing. When I was the CEO of the Dream Center in Los Angeles, a volunteer army of hundreds of people gathered at our church every Saturday morning. They prayed and invaded the surrounding Hispanic community to serve the neighborhood residents in a program called "Adopt-A-Block."

President George W. Bush called this the "army of compassion" when he visited our mega-church during his Presidential campaign. It was one of the many points of light that inspired him to launch his faith-based initiative and the Volunteer Corp. The Dream Center depended largely on the five thousand volunteers who came from churches across the country to serve the poor in Los Angeles.

It was affectionately called the "Dream Center" because thousands of people with broken lives and shattered dreams were restored in this giant complex, which was once the Queen of Angels Hospital. They included former alcoholics, drug addicts, prostitutes, gang members, runaway teens, even a few fallen celebrities like Jim Bakker, the famous television evangelist.

The facility was located in a gang-infested neighborhood where drive-by shootings and gang fights were a part of everyday life. You can imagine the reactions of elderly ladies when they peeped through their iron-barred windows to see a bunch of "blacks" and "gringos" standing at their door, looking like escaped inmates. In the beginning, they pretended like no one was home.

This program was the brainchild of Pastor Mathew Barnett who cofounded the Dream Center with his father Pastor Tommy Barnett. His dream was to pioneer a "church that never sleeps," a church that meets people's needs and opens its doors 24 hours a day, seven days a week. He taught his congregation not only to go to church, but to take church to the people. Every Sunday, we worshipped God in church and heard the preaching of the Word. Every

Saturday, we practiced what we learned by loving our neighbors through faithful service to the people in the community.

The volunteers invaded the neighborhood with black plastic bags to pick up litter, and believe me, there was plenty of trash to go around in downtown L.A.! We removed torn couches and discarded old furniture that even the garbage collectors would not touch. Sometimes, we painted over graffiti and mowed lawns that had more weeds than grass.

In the beginning, many of the residents were skeptical about our motives. Soon, the word got around the neighborhood that we really weren't trying to "sell" them anything. Persistence broke down resistance, and soon the gang members who had staked out every corner in the neighborhood warmed up to us. When their own mothers and sisters told them we were okay, they became our friends.

After five years, the program spread to a 50-block area around the church and exploded into the national spotlight as out-of-town volunteers took it home with them.

GOD STRETCHES OUR VISION

One day, God stretched our vision and planted an outrageous idea in our hearts about how to celebrate the coming of the new millennium. Because it would be the 2000th birthday of His Son Jesus Christ, what would happen if we shared his love by visiting every home in a five hundred-block area with a gift and a message of love during Christmas?

What would happen if we delivered a Christmas package of food, toys, and candies to every home and asked them whether they needed prayer? What would happen if we asked them whether they would like to receive the real Christmas gift of God—Jesus Christ?

It sounded like a terrific idea until we started thinking about the cost and the logistical nightmare of acquiring, packaging, and delivering *two hundred thousand* presents all in one day! Five hundred blocks of Los Angeles is bigger than many small cities in America. It would take a volunteer army of thousands, a fleet of twenty-five trucks and a budget of millions to make this dream a reality.

How do you get three thousand people to volunteer on December 23, when everyone is busy doing their last-minute Christmas shopping? How do you get a warehouse on such short notice? How do you raise millions of dollars in less than three months? Where do you get the extra staff that it takes to make all this happen?

As CEO, I was responsible for the answers to these practical questions, if we were going to follow God's call. But all I could see was a giant mountain with obstacles piled on top of obstacles before me. When we are really close to a new BIG challenge, it is easy to feel overwhelmed by its sheer size. It can tower over us until it totally blocks our vision of what is beyond, but God can amazingly restore our distorted sense of perspective.

I got on my knees and sought God for answers. When He spoke to me, I realized what I was doing wrong. I had been magnifying the mountain and it had grown bigger with every worrying thought. But when I focused on God and meditated on His call, I regained my spiritual vision and restored a healthy sense of perspective.

God gave our church the challenge and opportunity to touch and transform more lives for eternity; we were presented with the possibility of effecting dramatic change in just one day. We could provide a once-in-a-lifetime, turn-of-the-century event for volunteers in Los Angeles to live out their faith. People would be asked to give their time and money to bless those who were less fortunate and thereby experience the true joy and meaning of Christmas.

God Honors Faith

We exercised our faith by praising, worshipping, and thanking God for his divine "call," and we *trusted* Him to provide the people and provisions for this God-sized project, even though we had no clue how He was going to do that. The more we prayed and acted on the invitation of God, the more confident we felt about *victory* because the battle is the Lord's. We had learned to *magnify* our God and next to the size of our God, our fears began to subside and the magnitude of our problems began to shrink. Then, miracles started to happen!

First, a Reverend David Jessen was convinced that God had spoken to him about serving at the Dream Center. He was so sure that he had heard from God that he wouldn't take no for an answer, and he determined to move his wife and family at his expense to work for no pay. David was not just another volunteer; he was a former corporate executive and later the founder and president of a successful ministry that provided millions of dollars of food to the poor in Delaware.

Instantly, I recognized he was the bulldozer that God sent to help remove the mountain before us. I immediately appointed him as the project leader. When God calls and we obey in faith, He provides the answers, the people, and the provisions we need to fulfill His purpose.

We began to organize using a pert chart that hung ten feet high and six feet wide in the conference room. It listed the responsibilities of every team member and the days remaining to accomplish those responsibilities. It was clear to everyone that God had sent a logistical genius to help us coordinate this massive campaign, but what we did not expect was the next series of miracles.

Through David's contacts, God provided over two million dollars worth of donated food, toys, and candies for Christmas, sparing us from having to raise the money to pay for these presents. Then we received permission to use a vacant warehouse at no cost where we could store and package the gifts using a massive assembly line. This flattened the financial mountain before us and paved the way for victory. But there was still another mountain that could potentially sink the project. It was the final cliff-hanger. Could we get three thousand volunteers to deliver two hundred thousand packages so close to Christmas? Will God take care of that too?

It was no coincidence that our vice president of marketing had previously worked on Promise Keeper's Million Man March. On the day of our event, not only did we have the three thousand volunteers, but we were also swamped by the press and media. It was an event at which CNN and every television station in L.A. turned up, with their cameras and reporters.

During the night before, an army of people worked around the clock and up to the last minute to pack the presents in giant crates. Enduring the winter cold, people guarded the crates on the street corners all night long until other volunteers arrived the following morning.

When "D-Day" finally arrived, every one of the two hundred thousand presents was delivered in just five hours! But we never expected the surprise harvest—six thousand people accepted Jesus Christ as their Lord and Savior that day!

God always honors our faith. He gives grace to those who trust Him enough to pray and act upon His call. Then He answers our prayers and sends the people and provisions we need to fulfill His purpose. When we talk with God and enter into His presence, we realize He is much bigger than our minute minds can imagine. He gets bigger when we discover more about Him. When we meditate on the size of our infinite God, our problems shrink next to a BIG God.

WE ARE WHAT WE THINK

The truth is, we are what we think; we become what we think; and whatever we think about expands in size. That is why *right thinking* is so important.

When we *worry*, we are thinking about the obstacles and the troubles confronting us. We appraise the problems over and over again until we make mountains out of a molehills. Little doubts soon grow into giant fears as we process them in our minds.

But when we *pray* and focus on God, we meditate on the truth of who He is—a God who is sovereign, all-powerful, all-knowing, and always present. Praying magnifies God while worrying amplifies our problems; praying ushers in love and peace while worrying fans the flame of doubt and fear—the enemies of love.

The *Kingdom of God* is truly *within* us (see Lk. 21:17b).

If we control our thoughts, we control our actions; if we control our actions, we control our lives. It all starts with the content and procession of our thoughts.

HOW BIG IS YOUR GOD?

So how BIG is your problem?

That depends on the size of your solution. *The magnitude of your problem is inversely in proportion to the size of your God.*

So how BIG is your GOD?

That depends on how much you know Him. *The size of your God is directly proportionate to how much you know Him, and that is dependent on how much time you spend discovering Him.*

When you develop intimacy with God over time, you receive *ever-expanding* knowledge about Him. It will continually stretch and extend your understanding, appreciation, and trust in Him. His wisdom is like the intergalactic space where there is no beginning and no end.

God is big! He is really BIG! He is really, REALLY BIG!

Think how big this world is, then imagine all the stars in all the galaxies. If you would put them all together in one place, they would appear to God like tiny particles of sand on an endless beach that stretches all the way along the Pacific and Atlantic coasts of America. Even that doesn't begin to describe how BIG God is.

He is great, He is grand, He is gigantic, He is colossal, He is enormous, He is...infinite!

He is sovereign, supreme, immanent, transcendent, and He has no limits—that's why He is GOD!

He can help you overcome any obstacle, conquer any enemy, and remove any mountain that is blocking the path to His divine purpose and sacred destiny for your life.

How to Be A No-limit Person

When you know and trust a no-limit God, you become a no-limit person. He who can overcome his problems has no limits to his personal potential for growth and success in life. You will stop telling God about the size of your problems and start telling your problems about the size of your God.

In this the Internet generation, we want instant cures and immediate solutions. As spectators of television, we believe there is always a product, a pill, or a drug for every problem we face in life. However, these medicines only deal with the symptoms of our pain, not the root causes of our problems. "Self-medications" such as alcohol, drugs, cigarettes, chocolates, pornography, and shopping sprees numb our senses temporarily but do not heal the inner wounds of our soul.

If we agree that our problems are caused by *erroneous* thinking, then our solutions can only come through *corrected* thinking; no other external prescriptions, not even visits to the psychiatrist, will do the job for us without our will to change.

The truth is—*no one can change us except ourselves; nothing can change us without our permission—not even God!*

If you want to overcome the challenges in your life and need your burdens lifted, set aside quiet time to seek and communicate with God. He has the answers! He can change your thinking and it will change your actions. It will change the course of your life.

> *Nothing is impossible with God. The more you know Him, the bigger He gets!*
> *The magnitude of your problems diminishes in comparison to the size of your God.*

The quote by Oliver Wendell Holmes at the beginning of the chapter is appropriate for the Christian life: "Man's mind stretched to a new idea never goes back to its original dimension." So once you've discovered the size of your God, He'll never get any smaller. He'll only get bigger in time, as you explore more of Him through experience.

Through prayer and meditation, you will find the key that unlocks the door to the secret chambers of your heart. You will discover God's holy presence deep within you. He wants to give you answers to your problems and solutions to your dilemmas. If you seek Him, you will find Him; if you knock, He will open the door. And if you ask, it will be given to you because He promised this in His Word. (See Matthew 7:7.)

Have you been looking for answers in all the wrong places? Then look to God!

God is not in a box—He is not in a church. He is not on a shelf to be dusted off when you need answers. Look no further— the Kingdom of God is *within* you!

So what are you waiting for? God has been patiently waiting for you all this time. Take your journey within to discover the true God who lives inside you.

Then you will uncover the ultimate peace.

CHAPTER 5

ALL I ASK OF YOU

"Because he loves Me," says the Lord,
*"I will rescue him; I will protect him,
for he acknowledges My name.
He will call upon Me, and I will answer him;
I will be with him in trouble,
I will deliver him and honor him.
With long life will I satisfy him
and show him My salvation."*

(Psalm 91:14)

If you want to trust God…

SECRET #5: Love God—that's all He asks of you.
Then you'll experience the miracle of His
healing love.

BECAUSE HE LOVES ME

Do you want to know the real secret to trusting God?

Just love Him because that's all He asks of you. Then you'll experience the miracle of His healing love.

When God promised in Psalm 91:14 "*I will rescue him, I will protect him*," it isn't because we are worthy or deserving of it. He didn't say, "If you obey my word and carry out my instructions, I will rescue you and protect you."

God promised to rescue and protect us, "because he loves Me" and "he acknowledges My name." He does it because we love Him, we belong to Him when we acknowledge His name, like a child to his father.

When God said, "*He will call upon Me, and I will answer him, I will be with him in trouble, I will deliver him and honor him*," it isn't because we have passed His test of holiness through our complete submission, or that we have successfully completed our mission because of our perfect obedience. It isn't because of our faithfulness or good works. It is only "because he loves Me."

More often than not, it is precisely because of our imperfect obedience, our sins which cause us to miss the mark of His perfect will for us, that got us into trouble in the first place. That is the reason why we have to call upon God to rescue us. But in spite of our sinfulness and rebellion, He promises to "rescue, protect, answer, deliver… and even honor us," simple "because he loves Me…and acknowledges My name."

If that weren't enough, God promised to go even beyond that, "*With long life will I satisfy him and show him My salvation*." He promises to take care of us during this lifetime by protecting us so we can have long life, and satisfying us with the desires of our heart. Then He went all the way, even beyond this lifetime to show us the way to eternal life with Him through "MY salvation."

God's "salvation" came in the form on His one and only Son Jesus Christ. By the ultimate sacrifice of Jesus, the most precious part of Himself, God testified to His incomparable, indescribable, incomprehensible, unconditional, unfailing, perfect love for all time and all people.

God is our Father in Heaven and what He wants more than anything else is for His children to love Him—that's all He asks of us!

Why? Is it because He needs our love? Is it because God is "codependent"?

IS GOD "CODEPENDENT"?

Isn't it a bit egocentric for God to command us to place Him on a pedestal and worship Him? Isn't it a bit neurotic to demand that we love Him above everything else—with all our heart and with all our soul and with all our strength? Isn't it a bit "self-centered" to devote four of the top Ten Commandments to Himself?

If God is a God of love, and true love is always unconditional, then isn't it paradoxical that God would set so many conditions in His Ten Commandments and in Scriptures? Do we have to get a passing grade on these "religious" tests, before we can earn God's love? How "holy" do we have to become before we can enter into His "holy" presence and have a little communication with Him?

Why do we have to "love" God?

How do we "love" a God that we can't see, hear, or touch?

God is loving and the essence of God is LOVE. His love is pure, perfect, and without limits; it is unfailing, infinite, and eternal. God's love is unfathomable to the human mind because it is superior to any love man has ever experienced.

God is our Creator and Father in Heaven. Like any father on earth He wants to love His children and He wants His children to love Him. A loving relationship is only possible when two parties relate to one another; it flows two ways and is reciprocal.

God cannot give us His love, nor can we receive His love, if we refuse to have a relationship with Him.

God wants an intimate relationship rather than a superficial one, but He will not coerce us into it. He wants us to have the freedom to make our own choices. He wants us to share the details of our lives with Him willingly because God cares about every aspect of our lives, and He wants us to share each day, each night, each morning with Him. He wants us to share our lifetime with Him because He desires a close, intimate, trusting, and loving relationship with us, His children.

God's perfect love is like a fire—it is passionate and all-consuming! Isn't that how love is?

God knows that if this loving relationship is going to last, the feeling must be mutual and it must be expressed: "Say you love Me, that's all I ask of you."

If you want a relationship with God, do not be afraid of what He might ask of you. He is not asking for the sky; He is asking for your hand. He is not asking for the moon; He is asking for your love.

> *God is not asking us to be perfect so He can love us;*
> *He is asking to love us so we can be perfect.*
> *God is not demanding that we be holy; He is promising*
> *to make us whole, so we can be holy.*

This is the commitment of God's perfect love—a love that is like none other.

LOVE IS A COMMITMENT TO TRUST

Love is not a feeling. Feelings are fickle; they come and go like the wind. Love is a commitment. It is a decision to commit to trusting someone regardless of circumstances. Love is patient and kind. It is hopeful and persevering. It is giving and forgiving. Love is an unconditional trust and acceptance of the one we love.

God loves and trusts His children and wants to give us *everything* we need to live a good life. He demonstrates His trust by giving us the ultimate freedom to exercise our own will and create our own destiny. He proved His love by sacrificing the most precious part of Himself—His one and only Son Jesus, so we can be set free from the burden of our sins and be reconciled with Him.

God is consistent in His love, He does not go back on His Word, and He does not force His will on us. He allows us to exercise our will, even when it means we might reject that love freely offered to us. Sometimes, letting go is the highest expression of love. If you don't believe me, ask your parents…or just wait till you become one yourself.

Like a good father who prepares his children to face the world on their own, God equips us with a conscience that gives us an innate sense of what is right and wrong. He also creates in us a spirit that has an inner longing for communion with His Spirit so we can have a loving relationship with Him.

God trusts us completely because He is supremely confident that His goodness—His perfect love, tender mercy, and amazing grace—will draw us to Him, sooner or later.

God is self-sufficient and He needs nothing from us, He thinks of only what is best for us and is always watching out for our interest. There is nothing we can give Him in return except our love, obedience, devotion…and trust. If we give Him our hearts, He will give us the desires of our hearts.

God asks us to love Him because He knows that only His love can "save" us and set us free. Because God's love is the only perfect love there is, it alone can conquer our doubts and fears, heal our hurts and wounds, and correct our erroneous thinking that causes pain and suffering.

That is why He wants us to have a loving relationship with Him.

But He cannot give us what we need unless we trust Him enough to draw near to Him. His greatest delight is just to be with His children and to commune with them. A father's joy is never complete until *all* his children are home gathered around him. And that is God's eternal plan of redemption for humanity.

Sin and rebellion separate us from God, not because God has turned His back on us, but because we turn our backs on God. God's love is not vindictive or conditional. It is unfailing, unconditional, and eternal.

GOD DOES NOT CONDEMN US

Were you brought up in a very strict family background or did you come from an extremely "legalistic" religious upbringing? Are you carrying the burden of shame and guilt for something "unforgivable" that you have done in the past?

I have a simple revelation for you: God does not condemn us for our sins. Our sins condemn us, both in this life and after. We reap what we sow, and what goes around really comes around; but God has provided us a way out.

Sins separate us from God. When we disobey Him, our conscience tells us we have done something wrong. We automatically feel a sense of shame, guilt, and regret. After Adam and Eve disobeyed God, they felt naked and hid from Him. When we fear God's punishment, we have a tendency to flee from Him.

God's ego was not offended by this one act of disobedience. He was not looking for retribution nor did He desire to hurt Adam and Eve. He simply allowed them to experience the consequences of their own sins so they would learn to choose more wisely in the future. Through pain and suffering man would learn the difference between good and evil, obedience and disobedience.

They were deceived into wanting to "be like God" and God gave them what they asked for. They were given the opportunity to be "free" from God and were expelled from God's holy presence. Man had to leave his "paradise" and go to earth, and through the sweat of his brow he would till the land to feed himself; then he would die for his sin as God had warned in His Word.

When we sin, our conscience is temporarily numbed; but when we sin repeatedly, our conscience is seared, and becomes less and less sensitive to the prompting of our spirit. The more we sin, the more we violate our conscience and the further we drift away from God. This puts us in a vulnerable state where we open ourselves up to errors in judgment, deception, and delusions. We begin to confuse right and wrong, good and evil, until disaster hits one day.

C.S. Lewis said, "Pain is God's megaphone to arouse a deaf world."

It is not God, but the consequences of our sins or the sins of others, which impose the pain upon us. God's laws are perfect and His Word is trustworthy. He said He would repay us according to our actions, and if we sow the wind, we reap the whirlwind (see Hos. 8:7a).

IT'S NOT MY FAULT

It's almost fashionable pop-psychology these days to excuse oneself as a victim of circumstances. Just watch the courtroom testimonies of killers on the news. A lot of people blame their parents for their problems in life, or they attribute their neurotic behaviors to their childhood upbringing. Others find fault with their spouse for not meeting their needs.

Then there are those who hold their bosses responsible for being unfair, when they don't get a raise or promotion they had hoped for. They accuse their colleagues of playing politics. Some blame their friends and family for abandoning them in their time of need. There are even those who blame God when they run out of people to accuse.

Man inherited this disease of "excusitis" from his ancestors. If the first sin in the history of man was disobedience, then the second was his unwillingness to admit the truth. Instead he passed the blame. After Adam ate the forbidden fruit, he proceeded to blame "that woman" for giving it to him. Eve passed the buck by blaming the serpent who "deceived" her. It's the "excusitis" virus that teaches us to say when we run out of excuses, "the devil made me do it."

Blame is an endless and dangerous negative circle that leads nowhere. It is a refusal or an inability to accept and take responsibility for *what is*. If we live a life of blame, it will dig a hole so deep for us that we will never be able to climb out of it. It soon turns into a deep, dark, pitiful pit of futility—a living hell!

Acceptance of *what is*, is the beginning of wisdom. It starts by learning how to forgive others, then proceeds to discovering the power to forgive ourselves. Forgiveness is the cure for blame that enables us to assume responsibility and take control over our lives, to face reality and grow from our past experiences. Then we can transform obstacles into stepping-stones for a wonderful future.

Acceptance says, "That was another great lesson in life. There is no such thing as failure because I am not finished yet. Failure is someone else's judgment of me and no one else has the key to my mind except my Creator and me. God does not judge me, He loves me." This is the pattern of continuous learning and growth that God wants to establish in our lives.

The next time someone gets under your skin and starts judging you, don't snap at them in anger, "It's none of your ____ _____ business." That reply is judging them in return, and it only starts an endless cycle of antagonistic arguments. Instead, say to yourself quietly, "What you think of me is really none of *my* business!"

If you allow the judgment of others to seep into your inner spirit, you will start condemning yourself. Self-condemnation is the cancer of the soul that will eventually destroy your self-esteem. Psychologists have identified through numerous scientific studies, that low self-esteem and poor self-image are two of the primary causes of most problems people develop in life.

God knows that sin weakens our conscience, undermines our self-image, and eats away at our self-esteem. He sees that many of His children are trapped from birth, by the sins of others and by their own mistakes. They have no way out, unless He sets them free.

That's why God says, "Love Me. That's all I ask of you because My love will set you free."

THE HEALING POWER OF LOVE

Love is the only thing that conquers low-self esteem and poor self-image. Love is the antidote for doubt and fear, and perfect love casts out all fears.

Fear is the enemy of love. Hatred, envy, and jealousy are all birthed out of fear—fear of lack, loss, abandonment, and betrayal; fear of failure that quickly turns into the fear of trying and the fear of success. Then there is the ultimate fear that hangs over our head—the fear of death and dying!

God gives us the antidote for fear—it is His perfect and unconditional love. He promises us that if we will simply love Him and reach out our hand to receive, He will heal us, make us whole, and set us free from our past. He will give us eternal life with Him, so even the threat of death and dying cannot frighten us anymore.

God is outrageously in love with you and longs to be with you in the beauty of an intimate relationship. He descended to earth in the form of man to demonstrate His love through Jesus. He not only healed the sick, but restored those who suffered from low self-esteem—prostitutes, tax collectors, the poor, lepers, and anyone who was despised by those around them.

After His short mission was completed, He promised that *anyone can receive His healing love.* The only condition is we must *believe* Him. Before He returned to Heaven, He promised to send His Holy Spirit to anyone who wants a loving relationship with Him. He would be their helper, guide, teacher, comforter, and best friend. He would help them through their journey of life, until their spirits return to spend eternity with Him.

This is why the gospel of Jesus Christ is called the GOOD NEWS! He is our salvation because He is our "way out" and our *only* way out. It is God's greatest gift to mankind because we are not asked to struggle all alone in futility. We are not expected to go through life on our own strength. We are not alone because He is there for us, to help and heal us through His unfailing love.

God is saying, "Love Me—that's all I ask of you."

Love Is an Action

Love is not love until it is expressed and demonstrated. You cannot think that you love someone in your heart, yet do nothing about it. Love is an action; not a thought. It starts as a thought but when it conceives, it gives birth to words, actions, and deeds, expressing the depth and degree of the love. The greater value we place on that love, then the greater the passion, the bigger the personal sacrifice, and the deeper the demonstration of love.

God expressed the depth of His love, not only in words but by deeds. He demonstrated the degree of His love by showing us the ultimate form of giving—the sacrifice of the most precious part of Himself, His one and only Son, as His gift to us that we would understand. Giving is the supreme expression of love. "For God so loved the world that He gave…" (Jn. 3:16).

This is how God loves us, whether we know Him or not, whether we love Him or not. It is unconditional love and through this perfect love, He draws us to Himself. In the circle of His love, He teaches us to love our neighbors like He loves us.

When we learn and practice this secret of expressing love, we become more loving ourselves. As we become more loving like God, we become more lovable. Because so many people do not love themselves; they present themselves as *unlovable*, thus experiencing even greater rejection.

As we receive the love of God, we learn to express the love of God. Whether the object of our love responds or not, it does not change the miraculous metamorphosis that happens to our heart.

LIFTING THE BURDEN OF RELIGION

When God gave the Ten Commandments, His intention was not to control man, but to protect him from hurting himself and one another through sin. But "religion" elaborated and expanded on God's basic moral principles and guidelines until they became a set of man-made laws that in turn became an offensive burden to the people.

Instead of healing people from sin, which causes poor self-esteem, the laws made them more conscious of their sinfulness and added to their guilt and poor self-image. It was like rubbing salt into a wound, and the resulting sense of shame and condemnation alienated people further from God.

God came in the human form of Jesus to clarify His will and lighten our load. He reminds us that the main thing is to focus on the main thing—LOVE! Jesus reduced the law to just two commandments: Love the Lord your God with all your heart, with all your soul, with all your strength, and with all your mind…and love your neighbor as yourself (see Lk. 10:27).

He established the golden rule so everyone can understand and remember: "Do unto others as you would have them do unto you" (see Mt. 7:12). Now the essence of God's will is reflected in the perfect clarity of these very powerful and concise statements.

This is how God leads us back into His circle of love. First, He knows that unless we love Him, we cannot receive love from Him. Without His love, we cannot be made whole and holy; without His healing love, we are not able to give love to our neighbors.

You can't give away what you don't have. You can't effectively give love until you have passionately received love first.

But if we have a loving relationship with God, he resuscitates our life and creates a channel for His redemptive love to flow to us in healing power. As it fills us, it overflows through us to heal others in our hurting world. It is this spiritual nuclear fission of love that multiplies without end, and it all starts by accepting the love of God through the gift of Jesus.

WHO ARE YOU "IN LOVE" WITH?

Have you ever been "in love"?

When you are in the presence of the one you love, you feel GREAT! Why?

You feel better about yourself because of their acceptance, appreciation, and trust in you. Everyone desires to be accepted for just who they are. God's love is like that; He heals the hurts, wounds, and scars from our past so that we can feel whole again. In His presence, you begin to see with the clarity of perfect vision. You begin to experience an ultimate peace that makes you feel really good about who you are.

You are reminded that you are a child of God—made in His image. You wake up to the reality of the spiritual DNA within you. There is "divinity" in you and you can love not only yourself but you can love your neighbor as yourself.

> *When you trust God, you start trusting your new self—the*
> *higher-self and the God-self that emerges from the*
> *eternal, divine spirit within you. In His light,*
> *you see the light and become the light;*
> *through His love, you learn love and become love.*

Have you been looking for love in all the wrong places? Do you have an addiction to something or an attachment to someone who is harming your life? Are you suffering from "codependency"? Then know that God is the best co-depender you can find, because He is the only one who is infinitely dependable!

Once you experience the incomparable love of God, all other love pales, falling in the shadows of the brilliance of the light of His love. The world and all its temptations and desires grow strangely dim next to His radiant love for you.

Once you have tasted real love, any counterfeits just won't do anymore. Once you learn the joy and freedom in obedience, you will never go back to the pain and bondage of disobedience. That is why to love God is to hate sin.

THE CIRCLE OF LOVE

One day, God revealed His unfailing love to me in these words:

> *If you follow Me, I will lead you.*
> *If you obey Me, I will instruct you.*
> *I will never turn My back on you,*
> *Even though you turn your back on Me*
> *For I AM FAITHFUL.*

It is My unfailing LOVE that is everlasting.
It always conquers and draws you back to Me.
Therefore, learn to LOVE LIKE I LOVE YOU.

Let me conclude by asking three simple questions, and responding with answers that summarize how God's circle of love works.

1) How do you love God?

Get rid of your pride and the desire to be your own god. Turn to Him humbly. Come home like the prodigal son, but don't wait till your day of disaster. God doesn't ask for the moon, just for your hand, so you can receive His love.

2) How do you love your neighbors?

Get rid of your selfishness and turn to your neighbors with your hand extended to share the love of God that has been given to you through the gift of Jesus Christ.

3) How do you love your neighbor as yourself?

Love your *self* by receiving the perfect love of God that will heal your self-image and self-esteem until your "love cup" starts overflowing to your neighbors.

God says, "Love Me—that's all I ask of you" because "If you love Me, you will obey what I command...to love one another."

This is God's circle of love.

When you live inside God's circle of love, you will experience the ultimate peace!

CHAPTER 6

TRUST IS A TWO-WAY STREET

> *The knowledge of the secrets of the kingdom*
> *of heaven has been given to you...*
> *Whoever has will be given more,*
> *And he will have an abundance.*
> *Whoever does not have,*
> *Even what he has will be taken away from him.*
> (Jesus Christ—Matthew 13:11-12)

If you want God to trust you...

SECRET #6:   Be trustworthy. Then God will commit more and more to your care so you can have the power to change your world.

GOD TRUSTS YOU PERFECTLY

To trust someone is to confidently put them in charge, allowing them to do something without having fear of the outcome. It is a confident expectation and belief in the reliability of that person. It is the belief that the person has the ability to take custody of what is entrusted to his, as he exercises responsibility to carry out the charge of what is expected.

God has placed perfect trust in man as His highest form of creation—children of God. He made us in His image and gave us "dominion" to "rule" over *all* His creation (see Gen. 26-28 NIV and KJV). He gave us the free will to make decisions concerning our lives.

We are divine beings with the power of God living in us through His Spirit. We have the complete latitude to chart our own course and create our divine destiny. He gave us custody over everything, and we are endowed with inalienable gifts from our Creator—the ability to think, reason, create, and love.

God is perfect and He does not make defective parts. We are made perfect, whole, complete, lacking nothing from the start. Any sense of flaw or imperfection is simply an erroneous perception, flowing out of our illusions.

Do you think a tree would complain it is too short? Do you think a dandelion would wish it were a real flower? Do you think a sparrow would regret that its mother wasn't an eagle?

Only we humans find it hard to accept the reality of *what is*. This inability to accept who we are causes many of life's miseries. But the truth is we are wonderfully made. We have everything we need, once we realize that the Spirit of God that created us is within us. This Divine Energy who created us and everything around us, is also capable of creating the abundance we need in our lives, if we learn how to tap into it and let it flow through us.

YOU ARE A KING!

As God's children, we are given the responsibility, not only to rule ourselves, but also to rule our world. To do that, we have to acquire the wisdom, knowledge, and understanding to be good stewards of everything that has been entrusted to us.

*If we learn how to rule our **self**, we can rule **our world**.*
*And if we learn to change **our world**, we can change **the world**!*

When we trust God, we discover the power of self-control—the ability to conquer our *self*. As we acquire the strength to overcome our selfish nature, we establish God's rule in our life and in our immediate world—the tiny part of His vast Kingdom that He has given us to rule as *king*.

Our *kingdom* is wherever we can make a difference. For a mother, it is her home and family; for a business owner, it is his business, employees, and customers; for a pastor, it is his staff, congregation, and community; for a state governor, it covers his state and the affairs of all its people.

If we are trustworthy, God promises to expand our kingdom so He can bring more of "Heaven on earth" through us. For example, George W. Bush, former Texas Governor, was promoted to President of the United States. The American people elected him to lead their country after he demonstrated his trustworthiness as the leader of his state.

Start Where You Are

You may say, "Well, I'm not a governor or a president." But this timeless principle applies to whatever you are currently doing. God always works with us and uses us where we are. If we are faithful with a few things, He will entrust us with many things. Let me give me an example from my life.

In the 1990s, I was perfectly happy minding my own business as the CEO of a statewide public television network in Maryland. We owned six TV stations and produced programs that were seen nationally on PBS, and sometimes around the world.

One day, God spoke to me and invited me to *speak out* against the "misuses" of television.

Television is the most powerful and prevailing medium available to mankind. It is the "master teacher" of our time and the national baby-sitter of our children. Due to greed, man turned it into "an alter of seduction." Sex and violence became America's greatest export to the rest of the world. At that time, many concerned parents were outraged by Hollywood's unwillingness to curtail the increasingly offensive content that was corrupting the nation.

My first response to God was, "Who do you think I am? I'm only the head of one PBS network. Who am I to take on Hollywood? Besides, what can one person do anyway?"

But because I knew God had spoken, I obeyed. I originally thought I could pacify Him by going to the library and doing some research. I read some books on the subject but none gave me any inspiration; so I thought to myself, *"I've done my part; I'm off the hook."*

Then just a day later, as I was going through my mail at work, I found that Michael Medveck's incisive book *Hollywood vs. America* had mysteriously found its way into my in-box, with no letter attached to it. God started to speak to me through the passages in this book, and I became inspired...enraged and...on fire! This newfound passion spilled over into my monthly column in the program guide, which was sent to 75,000 contributors.

When my secretary typed my copy, she timidly ask, "Mr. Ho, are you sure you want to say that? Remember the saying: people in glass houses shouldn't throw stones."

This took me by surprise and I said, "Let me think about it." But in my heart I knew I had to obey God and speak out, regardless of the personal cost.

> *Trusting God requires that we surrender and submit our fleshly desires and worldly appetites and realign them to the plans and purposes of God.*

My willingness to obey led me to my next assignment—a newspaper op-ed piece which I wrote against television violence and its impact on society. Then I made speeches at various clubs like the Rotary and delivered a keynote speech at Goucher College. Remember, if we are faithful with a "few" things, God will promote us to "many" things. If we are trustworthy, God will entrust us with more so we can change our world.

What Will It Cost Me?

If you follow God, it will always cost you something. I thought my next assignment was suicidal. It was terribly risky for my professional reputation—like committing career "hara-kiri" before the whole world!

Every year, people from the television world gather in Cannes to convince others to buy their programs or invest in their productions. Situated in the heart of the French Riviera, Cannes is the "playground" of Europe. The name of the game is to find the most creative ways to upstage everyone else in an attempt to stand out from the crowd. After all, you are only competing with the *best* from the *whole* world.

There were the press conferences and receptions at the famous Ritz Carlton Hotel, which we managed to pull off the year before, and lavish premiere parties were held everywhere. Many deals were struck over cocktails on board glamorous yachts lined up at the harbor like sardines.

Up against giants in the business like Paramount, Warner Brothers, Disney, and the BBC, we were like grasshoppers! The year before we had accommodations at the Ritz Carlton only because of connections with our British partner. The classiest and choicest hotels were always booked up years in advance. Our sales booth had been so small it would have given you a case of claustrophobia if more than four people came simultaneously. We had no yacht to entertain anyone and could barely get a good table at the choicest restaurants where reservations were made days in advance. Everyone wanted to be seen with the right people at the right place and at the right time.

However, even against these odds, all things are possible with God.

This particular year, we were premiering our international series "Sea Power." Through our British partner, we secured a giant Russian cruiser to premiere this global series. Since the end of the Cold War, the Russian navy was all dressed up with no place to go, so it cost only $100,000 for our distributor to rent the cruiser. I think the Russian captain and his 450 crewmen really wanted to see what a topless beach in Cannes looked like.

When our BBC colleagues asked us in their impeccable British accent, "Why don't you chaps visit our yacht for cocktails and let's have a chat," my Cambridge-educated senior vice president replied in his equally perfect Queen's English, "Why don't you fellows pop over to our battleship tonight and have some vodka and caviar."

That night our ship was lit up like a Christmas tree, dominating the entire harbor scene. Everyone came to the premiere if only out of curiosity. Many thought we stole the show during that market. With the whole world of television in the palm of my hand, it was going to be a very special evening. It was to be the greatest moment in my career! I was eagerly looking forward to playing host, basking in the glory, and enjoying the ride of a lifetime.

HIS PLAN IS NOT OUR PLAN

But God's plan was not my plan—He had a different purpose. First, He had asked me to give up drinking right before this trip so I could summon up the courage to do what He asked next. To my amazement, He wanted me to deliver a "Jeremiah-like" speech during this premiere. God wanted me to throw a giant rock in a glass house and do it while the whole world was watching!

I was so alarmed with this assignment that for three days, I secluded myself in my hotel suite that overlooked the gorgeous beaches of Cannes. I prayed up a storm in the jacuzzi, which was bigger than a king-sized bed; the bathroom was bigger than a typical living room. I can tell you this: I never saw Cannes that trip but I sure got my money's worth out of that jacuzzi!

On the day of the premiere, I obeyed God and never touched a drop of the vodka, in spite of the insistence of the Russian admiral of the North Sea fleet. When I started to deliver the fiery speech, someone immediately began to heckle me in a foreign language. How rude! But how did he know what I was going to say? I knew immediately that the devil was trying to break my concentration.

With a rare determination, I finished my somber remarks, comparing the export of American sex and violence to the British export of opium to China that corrupted my grandfather's generation. I courageously called upon all public service broadcasters around the world to unite to counteract this alarming trend.

When I finished, there was a pregnant silence; I could even hear the sound of a wave crashing against the ship. The audience was powerfully convicted by my single, solemn, lonely voice of sanity drowning in a sea of commercialism. Only minutes before, everyone had been so boisterous with their brains pickled in vodka. Now their minds were sobered and their consciences seared by the truth.

I thought I would jump overboard and disappear into the ocean if that silence persisted for another millisecond. Then the Russian admiral clapped his hands together, and to my amazement, everyone broke out in a deafening round of applause. He honored me with his oversized admiral cap as a souvenir. The crew took it as a cue to exchange every part of their naval uniforms with the guests for some French currency. They were dying to go on land to paint the town red.

Who Do You Think *I Am*?

The next assignment was truly amazing! It showed that God can do anything. He can make a way when there seems to be no way.

> *If we are faithful with the little things, God will trust us with bigger things. If we are trustworthy, He will commit more and more to our care, so that we can have the power to change the world for Him.*

A Pennsylvania couple had lost their son to a tragic accident on the road. It was hardly your usual car accident; he died from lying down on a highway as a daredevil stunt to scare drivers. It was believed that he and other impressionable teenagers got this outrageous idea from a Hollywood movie. Several other similar incidents were also reported in the news throughout the country.

I was in a business conference in London at the time when *NBC TODAY* called to say, "We've heard about your views about television's impact on society. Would you come on the show tomorrow to comment on this tragedy? Brandon Tartikoff will represent the industry and you will speak for the other side."

Tartikoff was the president of the NBC entertainment division, a giant in the industry and considered a legend in his own lifetime. He took NBC to the top with such smash hits like *Seinfeld* and *Frazier*.

I was terrified. "Oh God, who am I to stand up against him? What do I know to be speaking about this on national television? I'm just not up on the latest proposed legislation in Congress regulating television. God, who do you think I am?"

Then I heard an echo from God, "*Who do you think I AM?*"

Within a few hours, piles of faxes flooded the floor of my hotel room. They came from the Internet and my attorney at our network, with all the latest proposed legislation and every news article known to man on this subject. Having access to this information left me no way out except to become an instant expert.

When I appeared on NBC TODAY, an ultimate peace came upon me as I called on President Clinton to appoint a national commission to make recommendations on how to curb the rise of media violence. As I mentioned before, he had appointed me earlier as the head of the public network in his home state of Arkansas when he was governor. I boldly sounded the warning alarm for the Hollywood community to exercise self-restraint before a lawsuit was filed by the victims of media violence, such as what had happened to the tobacco industry.

Trusting God requires that we trade in our doubts and surrender our fears. When I look back to see how far God has brought me since I obeyed His first invitation, I am convinced of this:

*God is not looking for people who are capable but those
who are available. Those He calls, He also enables.
He is not looking for qualified people;
He simply qualifies those He calls.
He can use **anyone** who will respond faithfully to His call.
He looks for obedient hearts and surrendered vessels that
He can fill and use to accomplish His purposes.*

HOW GOD REIGNS ON EARTH

God reigns as King of kings and Lord of lords over His Kingdom in Heaven and on earth. He reigns supreme in Heaven where His will is always done. There is no rebellion there because the rebellious have already been cast out of His presence. Satan and the rebellious angels fell from Heaven to earth, and man was banished from the Garden of Eden.

For God to reign on earth, He must rule in the hearts of His subjects once again. His truth and love must reign in the hearts of people so that His "will be done on earth as it is in heaven" (Mt. 6:10b). This is why He came in the form of man—to show us "the way and the truth and the life" (see Jn. 14:6) of how to reign, so we can regain the abundant life that we were meant to live in partnership with Him.

Our partner is His Holy Spirit who serves as our wonderful counselor, helper, teacher, and companion to guide us through life. It is a treacherous journey of reconquering "paradise lost." It is a journey of reawakening the truth of who He is and who we are *in Christ*. It is a resurrection of our spirit, an awakening of our God-self; some have described this as the "born-again" experience.

He knows our human weaknesses and vulnerabilities, and gives us the resolution to our man-made predicaments so we can overcome our self and be "more than conquerors" through trusting Him (see Rom. 8:37). Then we can manage our own lives and become coworkers in God's Kingdom, and co-regents over all God's creation.

HOW TO BE TRUSTWORTHY

So how do we learn to be trustworthy in God's Kingdom? How do we learn to become good stewards of what God has entrusted to us? How do we reign over our kingdom?

- We show trust, loyalty, and obedience to the King.
- We demonstrate character, integrity, and honesty in everything we do.
- We prove we are reliable, responsible, and diligent.
- We make the most of the time, talent, and resources entrusted to us.
- We keep our hearts pure and make no compromise with evil.
- We stand behind our word and exhibit honesty in both great and small things.
- We confirm that our ambition is not confined by our selfish desires.
- We affirm that we cannot be tempted by anything or bought for any price.
- We are not afraid to stand for truth even when it is unpopular.
- We stay true to our friends in good times and in adversity.
- We love our family and neighbors as ourselves, including those who are not so lovable.

How do you know this is what God wants?

First, He told us His plan in His Word; then He manifested that plan in the sinless life of Jesus Christ. Jesus Christ is our role model and His perfect life makes us certain about the Father's will so we will not be deceived. He confirms His will through His Holy Spirit, who communicates with us individually and guides us in our deepest being on what to think, say, and do.

Go back and carefully reread the list above. Check to see if Jesus lived up to everything on it. He lived the perfect life because God sent Him to be our model of what humanity should aspire to be.

God is perfect. He is a God of clarity and not a God of confusion. This perfection is revealed in the absolute detail and order of His creation. Just take a look around you and observe the precision of His handiwork in nature, or pay attention to the marvelous miracle within your body. Consider how 30 billion cells work together in perfect harmony. God does not make defective parts nor does He impart imperfect instructions.

POWER COMES WITH PRACTICE

The only way to experience the power of God in your life is to put His promises into practice and watch what happens. Spiritual principles and timeless truths can be taught, but they remain powerless words until they are lived and experienced.

We are not simply seeking explanations. Our hearts long for experiences that demonstrate the reality of what we have discovered. He revealed it to me this way: "When you are *faith-full*, then you will see my *faith-full-ness*."

When our faith is full, we stretch out our hand expecting to receive God's amazing grace. It is a spiritual *inheritance* that He has prepared for us. This inheritance is not comprised of earthly material things that fade away; the treasure is a bounty of priceless spiritual truths. This knowledge, when applied to life's situations, will set us free from the errors of our ways so we can fulfill our divine destiny and live a prosperous and abundant life.

An inheritance is not something we must earn. It is ours because of our birthright as children and heirs of God. It belongs to us right now! But we must remember that even an heir can forfeit his inheritance if he does not lay claim to what belongs to him.

We claim this inheritance by trusting God and accepting the gift of Jesus Christ. When we accept Christ into our heart, His spirit reawakens our spirit, so we can be reconciled to our Father in Heaven. Then our spirit can have communion with God through His Holy Spirit. We begin to see the truth of who He is, and who we are *in Christ*.

When we know that God is in us and with us, then we have the knowledge, courage, and ability to live the perfect Christ-like life with Him. When we finally know the truth, we no longer doubt; we are certain! It is this certainty that gives us the inner strength to change; it is this "knowingness," based on faith in God's Word and trust in His help, that gives us the power to *act*.

It is only when we act boldly on God's Word that mountains can be moved. Jesus says, "*If you have faith and do not doubt…you can say to this mountain, 'Go, throw yourself into the sea,' and it will be done. If you believe, you will receive what-ever you ask for in prayer*" (Mt. 21:21b-22).

LIFE IS A MOUNTAINOUS ROAD

Life is like a long and winding road. During the journey, we will encounter mountains along the way. What kind of mountains are you facing? Are you facing scarcity or poverty? Acting on God's Word will level your "poverty-thinking" mountain because God says He can do immeasurably more than you can ever ask, hope, or pray for (see Eph. 3:20). When you exchange your erro-neous poverty-thinking for abundance-thinking, you will start seeing and attracting abundance into your life.

Are you facing loneliness? Then know that you are not alone—God is always with you and He'll never leave you or for-sake you. Get rid of your "separation-thinking" mountain—you are not separate from God or from humanity. Your spirit is one with God and others; they are your brothers and sisters. If your immediate family doesn't accept you, connect to the larger human family you are part of. When you reach out and touch someone, you won't have time to dwell on your loneliness.

Are you facing guilt? Knowing God's Word will help you remove your condemnation-thinking mountain. God loves you; He does not condemn you. Only your sinful actions condemn you. So stop sinning and you won't feel guilty.

Are you facing anger? God's Word will teach you how to be rid of your "unforgiveness-thinking" mountain. You will never have to forgive if you don't blame in the first place. When you forgive those who have done you wrong, you will set yourself free from the self-imposed torture of pain, anger, and bitterness.

It all begins with correcting our erroneous thinking. To make this adjustment in our thinking, we must receive and act upon the Word of God. Scripture says, "Where there is no vision, the people perish" (Prov. 19:18 KJV), and "faith without deed is dead" (Jas. 2:26b).

Are you looking for vision? Are you searching for meaning and purpose for your life? Do you have a dream to live for? Are you seeking significance? Are you looking to make a difference in the world?

Look no further—God has all of it waiting for you. He is waiting to give you your inheritance—everything you need to fulfill His purpose for your life. But first, He wants to prepare you so you can handle this inheritance wisely and not squander it. He wants to train you step-by-step, day-by-day, to be a good steward who can invest and multiply it for the good of the Kingdom.

GOD IS PATIENT

God is patient and He allows us time to learn and grow. Through trials and adversity He stretches our faith and brings us to our knees, so we seek Him. Then he can bless us with spiritual treasures that are priceless—wisdom, knowledge, and understanding of God, and from God. This enlightenment sets us free from the prison of our own illusions and imaginations, defenses and denials, that prevent us from being able to conquer our *self* and rule our kingdom.

Jesus taught His disciples about trustworthiness this way when He said, "*Whoever has will be given more, and he will have an abundance. Whoever does not have, even what he has will be taken from him*" (Mt. 13:12).

He is saying this: When I give you spiritual treasures, use it or lose it. The way to keep the light is by sharing it with others. The way to have a more abundant life is by giving life, hope, help, and healing to others as Jesus did.

If we demonstrate to God that we are trustworthy with the small things, He will entrust us with bigger things. These "things" of God are not in material form but are the spiritual treasures of divine truths. We will make these discoveries when we learn the power of *faithfulness*. Then He can produce *fruitfulness* through us.

God will only trust us with as much as we can handle and no more. Otherwise, we have a tendency to hurt ourselves and fall prey to spiritual pride and greed. First, we must learn to control our *self*, then we learn to faithfully rule our kingdom. Then, He expands our kingdom gradually, as we learn faithfulness, trustworthiness, and fruitfulness.

God is patient. He builds our character slowly and steadily. He grows us like His mighty oak trees that takes years to mature, but will last through any storm. Man is impatient; we want it all now! We want to be like mushrooms that spring up overnight. Unfortunately, they disappear just as quickly when the sun comes out.

Therefore, do not seek to rush your destiny. It is an adventure of a lifetime, and there is a perfect time for everything under Heaven.

When you've learned to conquer your *self* and *rule* your kingdom, you are well on your way towards your ultimate peace.

CHAPTER 7

THE LONG AND WINDING ROAD

> *"Come to the edge."*
> *"We can't. We're afraid."*
> *"Come to the edge."*
> *"We can't. We will fall!"*
> *"Come to the edge."*
> And they came.
> And he pushed them,
> And they flew.
> (Guillaume Apollinaire)

If you want to trust God...

Secret #7: Believe in the One God sent. Then He can
           perfect you to fulfill your divine destiny.

WHAT DOES GOD REQUIRE OF US?

Today, many seekers and believers are struggling with a crisis of faith. They sincerely want to learn how to trust God and
obey Him. They honestly desire to do the right thing and endeavor
to perform good works as a way of pleasing Him. In spite of their

best efforts, though, some fall into the deep pit of disappointment and disillusionment during extended periods of adversity.

We come from a society of doers and we define ourselves by what we *do*. But God is more concerned with *who we are*. What we *do* flows out of *who we are*. Who we are is determined by *what we believe*.

When His disciples asked Jesus, "What must we *do* to do the works God requires?" Jesus answered, *"The work of God is this: to **believe** in the **one** He has sent"* (Jn. 6:28-29, emphasis added).

Believers believe in God and that He sent Jesus as the one and only Savior and mediator between God and man. Jesus taught His disciples to believe in Him. He said He was the *one* whom God had sent and stated, *"I and the Father are **one**"* (Jn. 10:30, emphasis added).

Jesus is part of the godhead. He is the Son of God and Son of Man, taking on the duality of both divinity and humanity. He came through a miracle virgin birth because God Himself is the heavenly Father of Jesus. He descended from the invisible world of the spirit and came in the physical form of a man on earth. He was the human face of God. He took on a different form in order to reach us at the level of our consciousness. Otherwise, how else could we understand Him and the mysteries of the invisible Kingdom?

God spoke His will through His prophets and provided knowledge of Himself; He then demonstrated those spiritual truths through the perfect life of Jesus Christ, which gave us understanding. He came from the Father filled with truth and grace to give us practical demonstrations of God's loving nature. Then through His sacrifice on the cross, He empowered us to live as He did—as children of God.

Jesus explained the essence of God in the form of the Father, Son, and Holy Spirit; all three are part of the same godhead, just as a human being consists of a mind, body, and spirit; or water that takes on three different forms: liquid water, solid ice, and invisible vapor.

The "mysteries" of God and the principles of the spiritual Kingdom were revealed through Jesus. He taught by using simple parables and translated timeless truths through stories of human interest that we could understand. Most importantly, He taught by example—helping those in need and washing the feet of His disciples, displaying the importance of servanthood.

His miracles were living and vivid illustrations, showing His divine power and human compassion. He explained that if we have faith, we too are capable of doing what He did, including miracles. Through our relationship with Him, we too are children of God. After He returned to Heaven, His Holy Spirit descended upon the early Church during Pentecost, and they received the power He promised and performed similar miracles.

Today, that truth remains as viewers can witness on television the miraculous power of faith, demonstrated in healing campaigns where thousands are healed by the power of God throughout the world. I have personally witnessed these miracles and have also experienced miracles in my own life, including the healing of a growing tumor in my wife's breast, which eliminated the need for surgery.

When believers *trust* God and take Him at His Word, God honors their *faith* by showing them His *power*. Life is a journey of faith, and it is God who authors and perfects our faith. The great joy in life is learning how to trust in a God we cannot see, feel, or touch. It requires that we go beyond using our physical senses and develop our spiritual sensitivity to walk by faith and not by sight.

It is a long and winding road that leads us to Heaven's gates. It is an adventurous journey, full of surprises and wonder. There are many times when it seems like we are strapped into a roller coaster and riding with blindfolds on. Let me illustrate this with a personal story.

PERFECTOR OF OUR FAITH

When my public television career ended "publicly" in the press, I thought it was the end of my world. Stories of my "clash" with the Governor were all over the front pages of the *Baltimore Sun*. They soon found their way into the *Washington Post* and radio and TV reporters were hounding me all day long for comments. The story had all the human interest elements to make the news headlines. It was a story about a whistle blower who charged that the governor was attempting to use the "public" network for "political" purposes. It was a clash between an underdog versus an eight hundred-pound gorilla.

At one point, both the Speaker of the House and the President of the Senate assured me on the phone that they supported me. I thought victory was within sight. A few hours later, that support changed as each of them said, "I am very sorry Raymond; you're on your own. Good luck!"

That day I learned a valuable lesson: In life, *might* often defines what is *right*. That is why the apostle Paul said, "Everyone must submit himself to the governing authorities, for there is no authority except that which God has established" (Rom. 13:1).

When my nine-year tenure ended, I thought I would never find another job in the industry again. Who would hire someone who was foolish enough to take on the most powerful man in his state?

I thought I had obeyed the leading of the Holy Spirit throughout the ordeal; but had I heard correctly? Was I not contradicting the Word of God when I stood up against the authorities? It all seemed so confusing at the time, but trusting God requires that we "lean not on our own understanding" (see Prov. 3:5); it calls for a leap of faith.

Real faith is trusting God in the midst of trials and believing when there is no evidence in sight.
It is holding on to His promises when there is nothing

tangible to hold on to and being certain about what God says
when there is no present substance to support that certainty.

Later, the chairman of the Maryland Public Broadcasting Commission met with me to explore a very generous "unofficial offer," which amounted to three years of the same pay with benefits. In addition, he offered me the chance to work under the foundation that I also headed, with a title that would be agreeable to me. The only condition was that I resign as CEO of the TV network and step aside quietly.

It was a very tempting offer for sure. I immediately called my colleagues for advice and talked to the president of PBS. I also reached Sharon Rockefeller, the CEO of the prestigious public station in the nation's capital. Sharon was the wife of a senator, former first lady of West Virginia, and former chairman of the Corporation for Public Broadcasting.

The advice I received from both these wise and politically savvy leaders was similar to that of my family, "Raymond, are you out of your mind? Just take the offer and run. You can always find another job; this is not worth it."

Ultimately, Whom Do You Trust?

The only one who was still open to other options was my wife who said, "Honey, you have to ask God and obey Him." So I prayed well into the early hours of the morning. In my heart, I was hoping that God would tell me to take the offer and resign; there would be financial security for my family and plenty of time to make a transition.

But the Holy Spirit said, "Do not take the offer, because you've done nothing wrong. If you resign without giving a reason, it will look like you are guilty. Stand up and fight for the truth."

Ultimately, whom do you trust? I had to choose between following God or man, listening to my heart or my head, siding with my faith or reason, listening to the Holy Spirit or my attorney.

110

Finally, I made up my mind to follow God no matter what the consequences. After I made a few more phone calls and found out that the commission was not aware of this "unofficial" offer, I politely turned it down.

A week later, I was summoned to a meeting with the Governor's Chief of Staff. The heat was turned up another few notches and I went from the frying pan into the fire! I was informed that the budget of the network had to be cut by over one and a half million dollars because of the financial conditions in the state. This meant that I would have to lay off many innocent workers, placing hardship on their families. It was obviously a political message, sending a signal to me—"Come to your senses!" But the Holy Spirit still continued to tell me to "stand," even when all the odds were stacked against me.

> *Trusting God is a demonstration of our unshakable*
> *confidence in God's goodness and integrity.*
> *It is believing that God will do what*
> *He says He will do in His Word.*
> *It is being convinced that He has*
> *the power to carry out His will.*
> *It is being sure that He knows what is best for us.*
> *It is being convinced that He will bring it to pass*
> *in His perfect timing.*

On the day of the board meeting, my fate was to be decided by a vote of the Commission, and the showdown was to take place publicly at high noon. The press was gathering outside like a swarm of bees next to a beehive. The tension in the air was so thick that I could hardly breathe, but God surrounded me with an ultimate peace.

That week, stories had leaked out to the press about my clash with the Governor. They pointed to me as the whistle-blower who alleged that the Governor attempted to politically use the statewide TV network to solidify his narrow margin of victory.

After the election, the Governor had awarded the chairmanship of the network to the owner of a public relations firm who had helped him with the election. But the reporters never investigated the substance or the validity of the allegations.

The truth is that throughout my public broadcasting career, I had remained politically neutral. During the election, I invited both gubernatorial candidates to my housewarming party as well as a 25th Anniversary Gala of the network. It didn't help matters when the trailing Republican candidate came to both events while the Governor declined. The rumors soon spread among political circles that I had been siding with the "religious right" since my spiritual conversion.

At the end of this long Commission meeting, I was asked to wait outside. The minutes seemed like hours. Then hours passed. Finally the door flung open and I received the verdict: By a vote of 8 to 1, I was asked to resign with no reasons given, and the sensitive subject of "politicization" of the public network was never discussed. The one dissenting vote was given by the vice chairperson who had earlier chaired the CEO performance review committee that had given me a good evaluation. I had informed her about the substance of the allegations, and she had encouraged me to bring it up to the Commission.

I thanked the commissioners politely and cut through the building, fighting my way past the lights, cameras, and microphones. Even though events had not turned out the way I had hoped, there was still an unexplainable peace surrounding me like an out-of-body experience. It was as if I was watching events unfold like a plot in a movie, except the events were happening to me and I was the tragic victim in the plot.

The next day, the reality of the situation hit me like a bucket of icy water. I was unemployed for the first time in my life! I had listened to the Holy Spirit and followed His instructions closely. I had tried to "walk by faith and not by sight," and now where did it get me? Where was my God now?

I was invited as a guest on radio talk shows and to my surprise, there was a groundswell of sympathy for me; even the previous Governor I had served for eight years spoke favorably of me. But how was that going to help? How was I going to pay the bills? Should I have listened to the voice of reasoning rather than this "Holy Spirit"? Should I have taken the offer and the money after all?

THE SECRET TO "KINGDOM MATH"

Let me share the secret to understanding "Kingdom Math." God is exceedingly faithful and excessively generous after we pass our tests. He always repays us for our obedience and returns to us what we have sacrificed. But that's not all—for the surprise factor, He likes to add an extra "bonus" on top so we learn to trust Him more next time.

Remember the offer I turned down? It would have been a $390,000 package adding together the three years of salary and benefits worth $130,000 per year. God restored every penny of that and more with His "Kingdom Math."

The first $130,000 came miraculously while I was unemployed. My grandmother died leaving an inheritance to her daughters. My mom passed her share on to my siblings and me. The second $130,000 came when Reverend Pat Robertson hired me to serve as Vice President of Marketing at CBN, the Christian Broadcasting Network. The third $130,000 came when I followed the Holy Spirit who told me to sell all my investments and buy stock in the Family Channel, which was owned by Pat.

I had some misgivings about those instructions when I first heard from the Lord. And I responded to God, "Isn't this a little too risky? The capital gains from selling my investments would really hurt, wouldn't it? Besides, isn't this known as insider trading?"

I called an attorney to be sure and was told not to worry about it. The Family Channel was a separate corporation from CBN. I had no involvement with it and was not privy to any inside information. Everyone knew The Family Channel was on the market and was considered a "hot" property by other major networks. The stock soared day after day and I made a $130,000-profit in just two weeks!

Now, if you follow the math, God had restored the entire $390,000 ($130,000 x 3 = $390,000).

I had a wonderful job in the work of His Kingdom, I was working for one of the most influential religious and political leaders in America; I was living in a beautiful home on the water of Virginia Beach; I had found my paradise lost and my ultimate peace!

However, just months later, after the Family Channel was sold, Pat called me into his office. He said, "Brother, it's time for a parting of the ways." I had heard about the management musical chair atmosphere at CBN, but somehow, I never expected that the changing of the guards was going to take place so soon! Only a few months before, Pat had given me the responsibilities of the president who had departed after less than a year. Now I too had the title of "former" before I barely got used to my new title and I was devastated! My trust in God was being severely tested once more.

It is in the midst of our doubts and fears, in the depth of our despair, that we learn to reach out to God through our spirit. It is in the valley of our "shadow of death" that we are forced to develop a greater and deeper dependence on Him. By humbling our *self* and surrendering our pride, with our hearts bowed down and heads lifted up, we look to Him and thirst after His presence.

In the intense heat of our desert crawl, we cry out in our desperation, "Father, I am thirsty for You. Take me to Your waterfall."

But in my depressive state, I complained to God, "Didn't I do my best for You? Look where I am again. I am at the bottom of the valley of despair. I am unemployed again. And I don't even know why." I saw myself as a poor "victim" of circumstances that I couldn't understand. I thought I had completely lost control of my life trying to "follow God."

When the stress and strain become almost unbearable, God knows our limits. He won't test us beyond our ability to bear. He sheds light upon our situation, penetrates our defenses and denials, stretches our patience and perseverance. Then we discover a new reservoir of inner strength and endurance that comes from this enlightenment.

Then God spoke to me, "*My son, have you already forgotten what I have done for you? Have I not restored everything...and more? Trust Me and you will come to know My faithfulness.*"

Suddenly, I woke up to the realization that God had revived my television career, gave me a chance to do the work of His Kingdom, paid me more than I had ever earned in my life. In other words, He had shown me the *glory* of God and His *power*...and I was complaining!

So often, just when we are ready to give up—like a kitten that has climbed up a mighty oak tree but doesn't know how to get back down, hanging on as best as he can for as long as he can— God releases, revives, and renews us. He surprises us by letting us fall, not to the ground, but into the palm of His loving hands. He makes a way through our wilderness and brings streams of living water into our desert.

Finally, I received an extra $130,000 from the CBN severance package. God not only restored the 3 x $130,000 = $390,000, but added another $130,000 as a bonus for my obedience, for a grand total of $520,000. This is the secret of "Kingdom Math." It multiplies!

Shortly after, He gave me another bonus when a former CBN vice president called. I had never met Him before, but we bonded instantly because we were both Ex-CBN Vice Presidents and we helped one another. He introduced me to a new job in relief and development. It started my next adventure serving the poorest of the poor around the world at Food for the Hungry.

Over the years, our faith gets stretched and strengthened, for God is the author and the finisher of our faith. And through experience, we gradually learn to trust God more and more. The natural outcome of that trust is to love Him more dearly, and follow Him more closely, day by day.

GOD BELIEVES IN YOU

Next time you go through a difficult trial, just ask yourself this question, "Would God allow me to face such a challenge if He didn't trust me with such a problem?" Adversities are opportunities in disguise; obstacles are the stepping-stones to change; and revelations from God are His invitations to change.

Trust releases our hand of faith to reach out to God and grasp His grace, turning physical stumbling blocks into spiritual stepping-stones. His grace is the spiritual "miracle growth" for our faith. It contains all the ingredients we need for our spiritual life.

As we reach out to God in prayer, meditation, intercession, and petition, He releases His grace. He answers the deepest desires of our heart and not our mind. He gives us what we need, and not what we think we want.

An unknown Confederate soldier expressed his experience of his journey with God this way:

> *I asked God for strength,*
> *That I might achieve.*
> *I was made weak,*
> *That I might learn humbly to obey.*
>
> *I asked for health,*
> *That I might do greater things.*
> *I was given infirmity,*
> *That I might do better things.*
>
> *I asked for riches,*
> *That I might be happy.*
> *I was given poverty,*
> *That I might be wise.*
>
> *I asked for power,*
> *That I might have the praise of men.*

I was given weakness,
That I might feel the need of God.

I asked for all things,
That I might enjoy life.
I was given life,
That I might enjoy all things.

I got nothing that I asked for;
Almost despite myself,
My unspoken prayers were answered.
I am among all men, most richly blessed.

God answers our unspoken prayers and blesses us at the deepest part of our being. In the shelter of His love, we experience the ultimate peace for our soul.

IT'S OUR FAITH THAT HEALS

When two blind men asked Jesus to heal them, Jesus asked them, "*Do you believe that I am able to do this?*" They answered, "Yes, Lord." Then Jesus said, "*According to your faith it will be done to you.*" Then their sight was restored. (See Matthew 9:27-30.)

The secrets of the Kingdom have been given to us—the Kingdom of God is within us.

"If you believe, you will receive whatever you ask for in prayer" (Mt. 21:22). Through trust, we claim what we need, knowing that even when it seems hopeless and impossible, all things are possible with God. He can make a way when there seems to be no way. He can pave a way through the wilderness, carve a river through the desert, and turn a wasteland into an oasis.

*Now faith is being **sure** of what we hoped for and **certain** of what we do not see* (Hebrews 11:1, emphasis added).

Learning to wait on God stretches our faith; it is a prerequisite to trusting God.

If you have learned the secrets to trusting God, you have developed the necessary patience, self-control, perseverance, and strength of character to wait upon Him. God uses the time of waiting to draw you closer to Him; to teach, revive, renew, and restore your perspective.

If you have been waiting a long time for your ship to come in, remember this: Abraham waited 25 years for God's promise of a son. David waited 14 years before he became king at 30, though he was anointed by the prophet Samuel at the age of 16.

Once you learn the secrets of trusting God, you'll become content in any and every situation. You can face life's challenges in peace because you know you can do everything through Him who gives you strength (see Phil. 4:13).

FINDING YOUR TRUE DESTINY

What kind of dreams would you pursue if you trusted and knew that God was really on your side? What would you try to do if you would be absolutely certain that you couldn't fail? Would you be content to go on, day after day, doing what you are doing? Would you not want to maximize your human potential and make the most of your life? Would you not dare to dream that impossible dream for yourself? So what is that something you have always wanted to do? What is the magnificent obsession of your life?

Are you tired of the superficiality and complacency of life? Are you bored with accumulating more as a way to gratify yourself? Are you fed up with indulging yourself with selfish pleasures? Are you worn out from chasing after success and lusting after approval? Have you had it with the rat race of ambition and self-aggrandizement? Are you feeling empty, lonely, and isolated?

Then perhaps you need to seek divine guidance and direction from God to find your true destiny. Perhaps your dilemma is not scarcity, but too much abundance. When all your basic needs are met, there is little joy in lusting after more of the same. It is like chasing after the wind.

Is it possible that the source of your discontent is because you are too narrowly focused on yourself? Why not try focusing on the needs of others? Your world and impact will expand dramatically.

There are so many people who need you—in your family and in your neighborhood, in your town and in your city, in your nation and around the world. They need what you have—your time, talent, and resources. God wants you to be His hand, His blessing, and His miracle. When you stop living for your *self*, and start giving of yourself, you will discover renewed purpose, passion, meaning, and excitement in your life.

THE PARADOX OF THE KINGDOM

The paradox of the Kingdom is this: When you stop striving, you'll start arriving. When you stop praying for a blessing and become a blessing, you'll experience a transformation in your heart. When you stop chasing after miracles and become a miracle, you'll experience a resurrection of your spirit.

Then you'll understand the meaning of the cross: In order to have a more abundant life, we have to give life. When we crucify our selfishness and serve others, we rediscover and reclaim our divine status as children of God. As Jesus showed us, we can call upon our Father in Heaven for power, provision, and prosperity to regain our paradise lost.

If you are spending a lot of time studying Scriptures and attending church, dedicating your life to prayer, fasting, and meditation, you have only *sought after* truth. The real excitement starts when you *live* the truth and *experience* the power of truth in action.

This requires that we stop clinging to the rugged cross and get on our cross; come out of our comfort zone and into the combat zone; get out of our prayer closet and into the neighborhood; get out of the pews and into the streets.

We have to be willing to deny ourselves, carry our cross, and pay the price of love as Jesus did. Only then can we become a fountain of hope for the hopeless, a source of help for the help-less, a balm of healing for the hurting.

When we bring reconciliation, restoration, and renewal to others, we've found the secret to our ultimate peace!

Conclusion

How to Become Fully Human

> Faith is to believe what you do not yet see;
> The reward for this faith is to see what you believe.
>
> (Saint Augustine)

Everyone has a spirit. We are all spiritual beings living in a human body. Everyone is spiritual because that is part of our divine heritage as children of God—made in the image of a God who is an eternal Spirit.

Goethe said, "If you treat an individual as if he were what he ought to be and could be, he will become what he ought to be and could be." Most people see what is; God sees what can be. Don't let others tell you who you are; let God make you into who He is.

To fulfill our highest human potential as spiritual beings, it is not enough to develop our mind and body; we must also nurture our spirit, if we are to be *fully human*. To do that, we must learn to live in union with our Creator and lay claim to our spiritual heritage. We must discover the secrets of how to live in open access to this spiritual world by trusting God. Then we can receive the wisdom, knowledge, and understanding we need to fulfill our divine destiny.

This requires that we live as pilgrims who are on a journey in search of God. It is a quest for the light and the truth. The journey begins by exercising our faith to seek God. We reach out to know Him through His Word given by the prophets. We gain knowledge of Him from the Scriptures, and we receive wisdom from Him through His Holy Spirit.

This process can only begin when we are reconciled to our Father in Heaven by accepting His gift of Jesus Christ.

Jesus is the most complete revelation of God,
appointed to be the way, the path, and the bridge to the Father.
No man can come to the Father except through Him.
There is no salvation except through Jesus.

This reconciliation process starts when we acknowledge we are sinners. We turn to God and away from our sins in repentance. When we accept Jesus Christ as Lord and Savior, we've made peace with God and we are reconciled to our Father in Heaven. Thus we begin our new spiritual life as children of God.

Through the empowerment of His Holy Spirit, He takes us on a journey of discovery. We learn the truth of who God is and who we are *in Christ*. Through the life of God flowing into us, we begin to receive the light of revelation knowledge expanding in us.

Our spirit is increasingly reawakened and our mind restored, revived, and resurrected to the truth of our divine heritage. We are recreated anew in the image of God, so we too desire to be like Him—to walk in truth and live in love. The ultimate purpose of God is that we be like His Son Jesus Christ and regain our divine status as children of God who can fellowship with Him.

When we trust God, we have access to the power of truth,
the provision of vision, and the prosperity of purpose
to live the abundant life He intended for us.

We begin to turn from our selfishness and loneliness that is based on a mistaken notion of our separateness from His other children. We learn the truth that we are all brothers and sisters of one human family, with the same Father in Heaven.

As our faith stretches through trials and tribulations, we discover an ever-growing inner strength within us that is capable of overcoming whatever obstacles that stand in the way of our sacred destiny. Through prayer and meditation, we tap into this spiritual depth inside the recesses of our own souls, and connect with the cosmic wisdom of the ages.

The natural outcome is a spiritual enlightenment and empowerment that compels us to care and share the light and love of Jesus with others. As we step out further in faith, making ourselves a channel of God's grace, showing ourselves trustworthy of this spiritual inheritance, God entrusts us with more and more spiritual treasures that He has prepared for us.

SECRETS OF THE KINGDOM

We finally uncover the secrets of the Kingdom—a spiritual paradox:

To find more truth, we must live in truth.
To keep the light we must be the light.
To receive more love, we must give love.
To have a more abundant life, we must give life abundantly.
*The **receiving** starts with the **giving**.*

Then we begin to understand the true meaning of the cross and the life of God. We start to walk in the footsteps of Jesus, the Prince of Peace, knowing that God has sent Him to show us the way, the truth, and the life. It is in Him, through Him, and with Him that we become fully human and live out our potential as children of God.

When we trust God and believe in the one He sent, we discover an ultimate peace in the midst of our greatest struggles, a peace that is beyond understanding.

Peace comes through trust, and trust is built on knowledge.
Knowledge comes only through experience with God.

*True peace comes only from knowing God through
the Prince of Peace.*

Are you looking for peace in your life, in your family, and in
your world?

*When you know the Prince of Peace, you will find
peace with God and man.*

Then you have found *the ultimate peace*!

Also by
Raymond Ho

HEARING GOD: THE ULTIMATE BLESSING

In a world filled with confusion, chaos, and crisis, it is the ultimate blessing to be able to hear God speak answers to the perplexing questions that surround our lives. He is the source of all wisdom, knowledge, understanding, and truth, and He alone is able to meet the deepest cries of our heart. Raymond Ho reveals seven timeless spiritual truths that unlock the door into God's presence. He shows how you can tune in and discern the voice of God, and how to distinguish it from other false voices.

ISBN: 0-7684-2073-3

Additional copies of this book and other
book titles from DESTINY IMAGE are
available at your local bookstore.

For a complete list of our titles,
visit us at www.destinyimage.com
Send a request for a catalog to:

Destiny Image® Publishers, Inc.

P.O. Box 310
Shippensburg, PA 17257-0310

*"Speaking to the Purposes of God for This
Generation and for the Generations to Come"*